a
primer
of
verbal behavior:
an operant view

STEPHEN WINOKUR

Prentice-Hall, Inc. *Englewood Cliffs, New Jersey*

Library of Congress Cataloging in Publication Data

Winokur, Stephen, (date)
   A primer of verbal behavior.

   Bibliography: p.
   Includes index.
   1. Verbal behavior. 2. Operant behavior. I. Title.
BF455.W54   153   76-4989
ISBN 0-13-700609-8

Prentice-Hall Series in Experimental Psychology
James J. Jenkins, Editor

© **1976 by Prentice-Hall, Inc., Englewood Cliffs, N. J.**

Printed in the United States of America

10 9 8 7 6 5 4 3 2 1

Prentice-Hall International, Inc., *London*
Prentice-Hall of Australia Pty. Limited, *Sydney*
Prentice-Hall of Canada, Ltd., *Toronto*
Prentice-Hall of India Private Limited, *New Delhi*
Prentice-Hall of Japan, Inc., *Tokyo*
Prentice-Hall of Southeast Asia Pte. Ltd., *Singapore*

contents

Foreword   *vii*
Acknowledgments   *xi*

1
Introduction   1

Aim   *1*
Characteristics   *2*
Status   *3*
A nonverbal example   *4*
Definition of operant   *6*

2
The Interlocking Verbal Operant Paradigm   10

The wrong paradigm   *11*
Interlocking paradigm   *13*

Size of units of analysis   *17*
Indices of operant strength   *22*

3
Mands   25

Definition and paradigm   *25*
Why deprivation and aversive stimulation become controlling   *27*
Reminder of how reinforcers work   *27*
Diagnosing mands   *31*
Supplementary strengthening and the impure mand   *32*
Why do speakers mand?   *33*
Why does the hearer comply?   *33*
Deprivation and aversive stimulation as supplementary variables   *37*
The self as mediator   *38*
Anomalous mands   *38*

4
Tacts   41

Definition and paradigm   *41*
Reinforcement for tacting   *44*
Comparison of tact and mand   *48*
Why do mediators play their role?   *50*
Discriminative stimuli as supplementary variables   *51*
Distorted tacts: inexact correspondence   *52*

5
Extended Tacts   55

Two mechanisms   *55*
Discrimination and generalization in tacting   *61*
Degrees of discrimination in tacting   *62*
The size of the response in tacting   *65*
Abstractions   *67*
Do animals tact?   *69*

6
Audiences   71

Definition and paradigm   *71*
Address   *72*
Audibility and the audience   *73*
Audiences as response selectors   *76*
Multiple and concurrent audiences   *81*
Shaping by the audience: a personality effect   *82*
One's self as one's audience   *82*

7
Echoics   84

Definition and paradigm   *84*
Echoism in children   *87*
Echoism in adults   *90*
Some odds and ends   *91*
Hearing and echoics   *91*

8
Textuals   93

Definition and paradigm   *93*
Reinforcing textuals   *96*

9
Intraverbals   100

Definition and paradigm   *100*
How intraverbals are reinforced   *101*
Chains   *103*
Clusters   *107*

10
Multiple Causation

115

Problems arising from multiple causation   *115*
Misspeaking   *122*
Verbal engineering   *125*

11
Autoclitics

127

Definition and paradigm   *128*
Kinds of autoclitics   *130*
The autoclitic a "fudge factor"?   *132*
Ordering as an autoclitic process   *135*
Reinforcement history for autoclitics   *137*
Awareness   *139*

12
Some Implications

144

The hearer   *144*
Meaning   *146*
Thinking   *148*

Suggestions For Further Reading   153

References   155

Index   161

foreword

As Professor Winokur tells us in this book, for many years I have taught a course on verbal behavior at the University of Minnesota. Its ancestry traces back to Skinner's earlier classic formulation of behavior in general, including speech. Winokur took this course in 1962, and about five years later he sat in and listened again—from beginning to end; people do that with this class. I have never ventured to find out why, fearing it was because they could not believe their ears the first time. This book reassures me; it shows that the operant analysis of verbal behavior *can* and *does* provoke and sustain thought. What's better—it survives continuing, informed reflection and a critical second listen.

Winokur has since taught a similar course of his own, and I am enormously pleased to see what the earlier, always incipient, formulation has become in his hands. He has found elaborations and consonances and clarifications that certainly had eluded me. No doubt there are more to come, free for the pondering to anyone who troubles to ponder. This point of view is something one can live with, and upon being lived with it will be seen to grow as if by a vitality of its own. One goes back to it and discovers new possibilities, new facets. It gives the psychologist an experience that is rather rare in our discipline—the excitement of *insights*.

I should think this book has something for everyone, in the best possible sense. For those already-committed to the ways of operant analysis, there will be the reassurance that verbal behavior can, (in spite of some recent critical harassment) still be considered within the domain of operant analysis—and here's how. They will be interested to see how the extension of operant analysis to a very complicated behavior class illuminates some familiar dogma without changing it—telling us what we must have been meaning all along. For example, the verbal case shows clearly that its controlling stimulus is inevitably involved in the specification of an operant, and therefore *must* be included in its definition; the operant is really not simply "defined by its consequences." Autoclitic behavior, a rich vein that will demand and then repay a reworking by the reader, teaches us something important about the interaction between stimulus generalization and response induction, and about how temporally concurrent variables can produce temporally successive responses. I should think it inevitable that someday we must all understand the autoclitic process; even nonverbal behavior has its grammar.

For the elsewhere-committed—the psycholinguist, the humanist, the philosophical rationalist—who want to know what the behaviorist's position on language really is—congratulations. To learn about behaviorism you have done best to come to the behaviorist. Here he is. His book will provide a clear and behavioristically sanitary account of itself. And it will no doubt be a revelation to you if your previous notions are due to secondary, nonbehaviorist sources.

I suspect there are few noncommitted on this issue. This is curious, since no doubt noncommitment and an absolutely open attitude of inquiry are the only sensible positions for any of us to take in these early times. Anyone who really believes, and then announces in public that he or she now has the final answer—the key to verbal behavior (or language, or speech)—simply *cannot* know what they are talking about. Speaking only for the view expressed in this book, I do think it reasonable to conclude that given what we *do now know* about nonverbal behavior, most of what this book says about verbal behavior nearly *must* be true. The Ultimate Science of Language, when it is written, will have much of this in it. Its errors are unlikely to be those of commission, because of the way operant analyses proceed. The sensible question is whether this truth, and truth derived as this was, is the *whole* truth. The behaviorist adopts the working hypothesis (it is not a claim or a theory) that the behavioristic constraints and economies are sufficient; if they are, his system will be elegant. Meanwhile he extends and purifies and corrects the system where he can, and as always with honest men, he watches for a disconfirming datum. Such disconfirming data, be assured, have not been encountered yet. All those brave new "proofs" of behaviorism's insufficiencies seem hardly to have drawn any behavioristic adrenin, much less blood.

The working-hypothesis attitude is the optimum, and certainly an excellent one for the reader to maintain here—*suppose* the behavioristic account to be accurate and sufficient. Taking full advantage of its apparatus without bending it anywhere, apply it according to its own rules to the domain of verbal behavior. See how far it will take you. *Then* make your bets. But not before.

You are in for a good time, and you may well end up at a destination you never expected to reach.

But first a *caveat* to the reader: what follows is titled a Primer because it lays out the structure of its argument in clean, straightforward, no-fat prose. It is rather formal and not very chatty. It is intended to be taken quite literally; we do not use metaphor. It does not elaborate greatly; it does not repeat itself nor underscore especially important points because, in fact, it makes almost no *unimportant* ones. All this makes for a high message-to-pages ratio; it cannot be comprehended in a quick read in spite of its brevity. And here is the caveat: the brevity and surface simplicity might betray you into judging that the book's ideas are as brief and simple as its prose. Well, don't. The underlying sense of the argument is rich, subtle, and sophisticated, as you will discover for yourself if you read attentively.

So, this short book is a favor to your time and pocketbook; it pays you the compliment of supposing that you will do some of the work yourself since you are given all the necessary systematic apparatus. You will find assertions here that do not seem to follow from what has gone before, but they do follow, and you should pause to figure out why they do, and whence. Some sentences will be counterintuitive; they are, however, products of the analysis. They are not necessarily wrong because they are at variance with "common sense," and I think, should not be lightly written off. If all this were nothing but common sense and ideas comfortable to it, the book would not be worth the writing.

The paradigms, or diagrammatic definitions of the functional parts of speech should be studied and fully grasped. They keep us moored to our basic operant origins and show clearly that no new stimulus or response variables, and no new processes, have crept into the analysis. The analysis involves only new combinations and complexities of already familiar variables that have been defined previously and that have become well-tempered in the laboratory with other species and other responses.

Kenneth MacCorquodale

acknowledgments

Office space and library facilities used during the preparation of the manuscript were provided by the University of Minnesota, California State University at Hayward, and Texas Christian University. I especially thank J. G. Darley, N. Livson, and J. Rosenberg for arranging these.

R. Boe, T. R. Dixon, J. J. Jenkins, K. MacCorquodale, and S. C. Winokur read the manuscript and made many helpful suggestions.

I am especially grateful to B. F. Skinner and Kenneth MacCorquodale. The first has been my teacher via his written verbal behavior, while the second has been a more personal instructor. I am greatly indebted to both of them for the material in this book. In large part, it is their book rather than mine. However, they should not be held responsible for any of its errors.

Saundra C. Winokur read the manuscript several times, typed it, fed and otherwise encouraged the author, and refused to be satisfied unless the account was made clear and unambiguous. Without her help, encouragement, and criticism, the manuscript would never have been completed. This book is for her.

1

introduction

For some readers, the first part of this book will be largely a review of what they already know about the work of B. F. Skinner. For other readers, this part of the book will provide a concise introduction to the methodology and philosophy of Skinnerian psychology. Both groups of readers, however, should give it their attention because it will enable them to develop a more critical understanding of the approach I will be taking to the subject matter of the rest of the book.

AIM

My aim here is to introduce you to Skinner's natural science account of an individual's verbal behavior. This account seeks to explain talking in terms of a person's past history, current circumstances, and nothing more. Another way of saying this is that we will look at an enumeration of the variables of which verbal behavior is a function. That is, you will be introduced to what Skinner, and I, consider a behavioral analysis of talking.

You may know that Skinner has written a book called *Verbal Behavior*, and you may have wondered why you aren't being asked to read that book instead of this one. I would say that many years of teaching experience have shown that *Verbal Behavior* is not organized in a way that makes it suitable for use as an introductory text. It also contains a lot more material than we will be concerned with here. After all, it is a complete account of the views of one of the world's most eminent psychologists on a very large area of human behavior. Skinner's *Verbal Behavior* includes discussions of writing and editing, as well as talking and reading. I'll just tell you about the last two. My approach here will be derived from that developed by Kenneth MacCorquodale, who for many years has taught a course called "Verbal Behavior" at the University of Minnesota. MacCorquodale began to teach his course at about the same time that Skinner was giving his William James Lectures (the forerunners of *Verbal Behavior*) at Harvard University. The course and the book are very similar; I cannot say which contained what first. No matter—this book is greatly indebted to both. The technical terms and the basic plan of anlaysis are surely Skinner's, but almost all of the diagrams and many of the examples were developed by MacCorquodale in his "pedagogical paraphrase" of Skinner during his lectures. I consider both men to have made important contributions to the account of verbal behavior, and to be excellent and inspiring teachers. This book is, then, an attempt to share what I have learned from them with you.

CHARACTERISTICS

I want to characterize this approach briefly by mentioning several salient aspects of it.

It is a STIMULUS-RESPONSE PSYCHOLOGY. THIS MEANS THAT BEHAVIOR IS UNDERSTOOD TO BE THE SUBJECT MATTER OF THE INQUIRY. THE REAL MOVEMENTS OF AN ANIMAL OR ITS PARTS WHICH ARE PRODUCED BY THAT ANIMAL'S MUSCLES CONSTITUTE WHAT IS TO BE EXPLAINED, rather than ideas, meanings, wants, desires, intentions, expectations, or any kind of hypothetical physiological mechanisms.

A NATURAL SCIENCE ACCOUNT IS WHAT IS OFFERED. THE SUBJECT MATTER CONSISTS OF, AND IS LIMITED TO, PUBLIC, EMPIRICAL, REAL, INTERSUBJECTIVELY OBSERVABLE EVENTS. Verbal behavior is behavior; it is not something different from nonverbal behavior. Making noise with your mouth (talking) is just as much, and no more or no less, behavior as is riding a bicycle. We will not be concerned with talking as "symbolic behavior" or as a "vehicle for ideas." This approach is not a popular one. Many scholars, including many psychologists for that matter, do not agree that what is to be explained is muscle movements or the noise that they produce. Some see these data as a basis for inference to minds, cognitions, plans, structures, grammars, algorithms, and so forth. However, we will not be concerned here with explaining those sorts of inferred entities, nor will we make use of them in explaining behavior.

In this account, the variables of which behavior is a function are sought among public, empirical, real, observable events. We look at present and past states of the organism (deprivation), his genetic constitution (a human or a chimpanzee can acquire verbal behavior, but a pigeon cannot), and present and past states of the environment (stimuli); all of which are real, physical, intersubjectively observable things. The covariations of changes in these empirical independent variables and changes in behavior may be described (stated). DESCRIPTIONS OF FUNCTIONAL RELATIONS AMONG EMPIRICAL VARIABLES CONSTITUTE THE SORT OF CAUSAL ACCOUNT THAT IS PRESENTED HERE. CAUSE, CONTROL, AND SIMILAR WORDS MEAN, WHEN USED HERE, PRECISELY THE OBSERVED RELATIONSHIP BETWEEN PUBLIC DEPENDENT AND INDEPENDENT VARIABLES.

A fundamental premise of this approach is that the basic terms and processes involved in the science of behavior are general and applicable to all behavior, even verbal behavior. We can do research with pigeons and rats to locate important processes and their effects, and then apply the results of that work to verbal behavior.

STATUS

At the present time we can give only a "plausible reconstruction" or theory of the origin, maintenance, and control of verbal behavior in these terms. The vocabulary and the laws come from laboratory research on other organisms (rats and pigeons) doing other things (pressing bars and pecking at plastic disks). But this vocabulary and these laws should apply to talking. Verbal behavior stretches Skinner's explanatory system to its limits. The approach taken here is to see how far we can go with a scientific account without resorting to entities or processes occurring somewhere else at some other level of discourse, that is, in the brain or mind.

If he were asked, I think that Skinner would say: Not only is this a proposal for an account of verbal behavior, it *is* an account of that subject matter; it probably is correct; it is supported by evidence; it is not *ad hoc*, for it can be further supported by new, not yet collected evidence; the account and the evidence are empirical, public, and observational, but mostly not experimental; that is, observations are made and data are collected, but independent variables are rarely manipulated—nevertheless, this is still empirical science, as much as astronomy and geology are empirical sciences.

Skinner does not, by any means, have the only stimulus-response psychology. There are many other approaches to stimulus-response psychology, due largely to men such as Hull, Spence, Guthrie, and Estes, to name just a few. Such other stimulus-response psychologies are beyond the scope of this book. Another approach to the study of verbal behavior which is also beyond the scope of this book is a relatively new type of psychology.

This is called "psycholinguistics" (for example, see the book by Slobin) and is based on the assumption that there *must* be something more to verbal behavior, and that any stimulus-response account *must* be inadequate because it leaves things out. This approach originated in linguistics and closely resembles Gestalt psychology in many respects, but most particularly because it has been a critical movement. I see no special advantage to comparing and contrasting psycholinguistics with Skinner's approach. If you read this book as part of a course, you may find that your instructor will make the comparisons. Or you may, once you finish this book, make them yourself. My purpose here is to explain this account as best I can, display some of the evidence for it, and let you reach your own conclusions.

A NONVERBAL EXAMPLE

Although Skinner's account may be claimed to have certain aims and characteristics, it may rightfully be asked whether or not such an approach is possible, and if it is possible, has it been successful. Can one really give a causal account of an individual's behavior in terms of his past history and current circumstances, where all terms, both inputs and outputs, are physically specifiable; and where inputs consist of states of the environment (stimuli) and of the organism (deprivation) and outputs consist of behavior (responses)? Can the account also be an exposition of the relationships between variables—a description of what leads to what—where all terms are general and not restricted to verbal individuals?

I claim that these questions can be answered in the affirmative, because many examples show that the Skinnerian program has worked. Let us look at a case where this approach has been eminently successful. There are several advanced accounts of this, as well as many introductions to it which treat it in great detail (see "Suggestions for Further Reading" in the back of this book, especially if what follows is uncomfortably new for you.) This is the part with which I guessed that you might be well acquainted. Even if you are, please let me review it.

Let us see how to give a natural science, psychological, causal account of the nonverbal behavior of a nonverbal animal exclusively in terms of his past history and current circumstances. To do this we follow Skinner's lead by finding a pigeon, and then putting him in a small box. Then we observe his pecking.

We may, as an aside, make a methodological observation at this point. We didn't act like the Nobel Prizewinning ethologists Lorenz and Tinbergen. We didn't ask what the bird does. We didn't survey its repertoire. We named a behavior unit (the peck) and asked, When does it occur? and What causes it to happen? We will do the same sort of thing with verbal behavior. We will ask what the circumstances are under which a man will say "cat," "uncle," "Grace me no grace, nor uncle me no uncle." This is a deliberate difference in approach. Neither we nor the ethologists are right or wrong; the aims of the two approaches are different.

Let us return to the pigeon. We see that if the peck at a plastic disk on the wall of the box (the key) is followed by the presentation of what is normally food for the pigeon, the pecking may increase. By manipulating the consequences of the bird's behavior we can cause or change (shape) the behavior's rate or frequency or its intensive properties, such as force, duration, or excursion (how far in space the bird moves). To be sure, the operations I have described work only if the bird is "hungry." They work automatically and regularly if he has been deprived of food, and they don't work at all if he hasn't. In fact, we know that if he hasn't been food deprived, say, just after a big meal, the peck goes away.

As you may remember, we can get fancy about this; fancy for a dumb bird, anyway. We can put a Christmas tree bulb behind the key and arrange things so that if the bird pecks when the light is on, food is presented; and if the bird pecks when the light is off, no food is delivered to him. After a few food and no-food periods, a "hungry" bird "learns." The pecking comes and goes with the light—given, of course, that he is deprived of food beforehand.

These seem to be the significant events:

Deprivation: the withholding of the food beforehand

Stimulus: the lighted key

Response: the peck

Reinforcer: the food

Contingency: the relation that we set up among the preceding items

The example seems to show a surefire method of controlling pecking. Not only that, we know that this method of conditioning works in almost every case, irrespective of the individual, stimulus, response, reinforcer, or species involved. The example is one of *operant conditioning*. There are limitations on this process, but we won't go into them now. Let us first review what operant behavior is.

DEFINITION OF OPERANT

What follows will be somewhat new even to those of you who are familiar with the writings of Skinner and his followers. The illustration below shows a paradigm for an operant. In this book I display the model case, or idealized pattern, for each important class of behavior, or each process, in the form of a generalized schematic diagram which I call a paradigm. OPERANT BEHAVIOR IS THE NAME OF A VERY LARGE CLASS OR GROUP OF DIFFERENT BEHAVIORS. THEY ALL HAVE CERTAIN COMMON PROPERTIES, THE MOST IMPORTANT OF WHICH IS THAT THEY ARE THE RESPONSES THAT ARE PARTS OF OPERANTS. This definition differs from the traditional one. Here responses are *not* operants. They are *parts* of operants. It should be noted that this usage is a significant departure from Skinner's way of talking about these matters and resembles the positions taken by J. E. R. Staddon and J. D. Findley.

$$S^D \atop OR \longrightarrow R \atop DEP^{\underline{N}}$$

$$\underbrace{}$$

AN OPERANT

Because this way of talking about operants may be new to you, let us now look at the components of the paradigmatic operant, starting from the right side of the diagram. We begin with the *response* (R)—the pigeon's peck in our nonverbal example. RESPONSES CAN BE DESCRIBED IN TWO WAYS. (1) THEIR TOPOGRAPHIES MAY BE STATED; WE MAY BE TOLD WHAT MUSCLES MOVE WHICH PARTS OF THE BODY, AND WITH WHICH FORCES, DURATIONS, EXCURSIONS, OR OTHER INTENSIVE PROPERTIES. (2) WE MAY BE TOLD THE EFFECTS OR CONSEQUENCES OF THE MOVEMENTS UPON THE ENVIRONMENT. Most operant responses are described in terms of their effects. For example, the bar was pressed, the rat entered the goal box, the key was pecked, the switch was flipped, the letter was typed. A response such as the bar-press is a class (set). It has members which are individual bar-presses. This is just like individuals who are members of a species (a man, the species man). We will see that reinforcement does not reproduce the individual response that it follows, but it does lead to a changed probability of members of that class. Our pigeon's individual pecks never return, but he does produce more responses of that sort even though each peck is somewhat different from the others.

S^D is the notation which we will use for a *discriminative stimulus*. THE DISCRIMINATIVE STIMULUS FOR A RESPONSE IS A STATE OF THE ENVIRONMENT THAT IS OFTEN PRESENT WHEN THAT RESPONSE IS FOLLOWED BY A REINFORCER. Discriminative stimuli are classes also. Not every occurrence of the light behind the key is exactly the same as every other one. Remember that discriminative stimuli are not CS's (the conditioned stimuli that acquire the power to elicit reflex responses in the procedure investigated by Pavlov). The responses under the control of CS's are parts of reflexes; operant responses are *not* reflex responses. Also remember that not every physically specifiable energy change is a stimulus for a given individual or species. Light is not a stimulus for blind dogs, nor are X-rays stimuli for humans, although photographs made by X-rays are. Although an animal may have the anatomical and physiological ability to be controlled by a physical energy change, it is not a discriminative stimulus for him until some of his behavior has been reinforced in its presence. A pigeon can see red, but he doesn't do so until a psychologist or some other part of the world feeds him for pecking red things and extinguishes (does not reinforce) his pecks at nonred things.

When we work with animals other than humans, we often work with a reinforcer that depends on *deprivation* for its effectiveness. Even to an experienced pigeon, food is not a reinforcer unless he is "hungry." You may recall that not all reinforcers depend on deprivation for their effectiveness; candy and other sweet stuffs work whether one is hungry or not. Notice also that deprivation is *not* a stimulus. It is a *procedure* that sometimes, but not always, produces some stimuli. DEPRIVATION IS THE WITHHOLDING OF STIMULI TO WHICH THE ORGANISM HAS PREVIOUSLY HAD SOME DEGREE OF ACCESS. They must be stimuli; if they aren't, there won't be any effect on behavior. If you withhold oxygen from a man but continue to supply him with "air," there is no effect on his behavior, but he dies. The requirement that an organism have some degree of access to the stimulus becomes clearer if we consider whether I have been deprived of Sophia Loren or Nelson Rockefeller's money. We would not normally say that I have, and the reason seems to be that I have never had regular or irregular access to either, even though both might be reinforcing. We may note a final peculiarity of deprivation; it is in one respect like a discriminative stimulus. When an individual is deprived, any responses reinforced during this deprivation may come under the control of the deprivation in that they are more likely to recur when the deprivation recurs, and less likely to occur when the deprivation is absent. This phenomenon appears irrespective of whether or not the deprivation produces characteristic stimuli.

THE ARROW IN THE PARADIGM FOR THE OPERANT REPRESENTS THE FACT OF CONTINGENCY OR CONDITIONALITY—THE RELATIONSHIP BETWEEN THE DISCRIMINATIVE STIMULUS OR THE DEPRIVATION AND THE RESPONSE. The operant, then, is composed of a *relation* between the antecedent conditions (deprivation or discriminative stimulus) and the response class. Instances of the operant occur when a member of the response class occurs under the control of a member of the class of controlling antecedent conditions. But the operant is a set (class) itself, with each instance of it being a member of the set. So, our pigeon's antecedent conditions were no food and the light behind the key being on. Its response class was key-pecking. Each occurrence of an operant was an instance of time-since-food (deprivation) plus light-on-the-key (discriminative stimulus) followed by a peck at the key response (R). And, each such instance of controlled key-pecks was an instance (a member) of the class of operants.

In the preceding I have mentioned the role of the reinforcing stimulus several times. The following illustration shows the relation of reinforcers to operants by means of a paradigm.

$$\underbrace{\begin{matrix} S^D \\ OR \\ DEP^{\underline{N}} \end{matrix} \longrightarrow R}_{\text{OPERANT}} \longrightarrow S^R \longrightarrow Pr\left(\begin{matrix} S^D \\ OR \\ DEP^{\underline{N}} \end{matrix} \longrightarrow R\right)\uparrow$$

The symbol S^R is used to indicate a *reinforcing stimulus*, while the symbol Pr ( )↑ indicates an increase in the probability of whatever is within the parentheses. Thus, the paradigm indicates that when an operant is followed by a reinforcing stimulus, the subsequent probability of that operant is increased. A REINFORCER (REINFORCING STIMULUS) IS ANY STIMULUS THAT INCREASES THE SUBSEQUENT PROBABILITY OF THE PRECEDING RESPONSE IN THE PRESENCE OF THE CONTROLLING CIRCUMSTANCES (DEPRIVATION OR DISCRIMINATIVE STIMULI). A reinforcer *strengthens* an operant; it increases the control exerted over the response by the antecedent conditions. The probability of emission of the response in the presence of those conditions in the future will be higher. The functional relationship represented by the arrow in the paradigm for the operant is made stronger. We may notice that operants do not exist before reinforcers have acted on behavior. The behavior may occasionally occur with a low probability, but the occurrence of a reinforcing stimulus following a response is what creates, strengthens, and maintains operants.

REMEMBER THAT REINFORCERS ALWAYS INCREASE RESPONSE PROBABILITY. POSITIVE REINFORCERS DO SO BY BEING PRESENTED AFTER THE RESPONSE; NEGATIVE REINFORCERS DO SO BY BEING TURNED OFF AS A CONSEQUENCE OF THE RESPONSE. REINFORCEMENT, THEN, IS THE PROCESS OF INCREASING OPERANT STRENGTH EITHER BY PRESENTING A POSITIVE REINFORCER OR BY TERMINATING A NEGATIVE ONE. The relation between reinforcements and operants is not always one for one. Reinforcements may be scheduled *intermittently* and thus produce very strong operants (operant strength is often shown as persistent behavior or high rates of responding). This is especially true in verbal behavior; no professor is reinforced each time he opens his mouth. Sometimes the response does not occur at all or does not have desired intensive properties (amplitude, latency, force, duration, excursion, etc.). In this situation, a procedure called *shaping* must be used. SHAPING CONSISTS OF THE DIFFERENTIAL REINFORCEMENT OF SUCCESSIVE APPROXIMATIONS TO THE DESIRED RESPONSE. In our example of the pigeon, if the bird didn't peck the lighted key, even though it was food deprived, we would have to shape keypecking. At first we would reinforce (by presenting food) any movement toward the wall on which the key was mounted. Then we would wait for head movements toward the key and reinforce them, but not other behaviors. Finally, reinforcement would be made contingent on behavior which brought the beak in contact with the key.

These are about all the terms and definitions that we need for this account of verbal behavior. What follows next is an imaginary dialogue which illustrates the *kind* of explanation that we give for verbal behavior, but does it for the key-pecking pigeon.

Q.: Why is that pigeon pecking the plastic disk?

A.: Because the light is on (if I turn it off, see, he stops), and he has been deprived of food.

Q.: But why does he peck when the light is on and he is hungry?

A.: Because in the past, if he pecked when the light was on, I gave him food when he was "hungry."

Q.: Is that all?

A.: Yes.

This example displays a functional view of cause or causal relationships. What is involved here is a specification of "what leads to what." That is, what events in the environment lead to changes in behavior? Further questions, such as "why does he peck if in the past when he pecked and was food deprived and the light was on, you fed him?," are for another discipline—physiology. *By agreement*, we stop here. There is plenty of work for us to do. The physiologists will explain, someday, what it is inside the bird that makes food a reinforcer to him when he is "hungry," and what it is inside the bird that makes reinforcers have the effects upon operant strength that they do. We will want to know about such matters, and fortunately there are people working on getting this sort of information. But, in the meantime, we can go ahead and find out what the psychological laws are. This will be helpful in forming a complete account of the way the world works, because these psychological laws are what the physiologist is trying to explain.

2

the interlocking verbal operant paradigm

What we now have to do is apply the general operant paradigm to the verbal case. We have the paradigm, on the one hand, and speaking, on the other. We have to see if we can fit them together without doing damage to either. To do so we will take the accomplished speaker, observe what he is doing, enumerate the ways in which discriminative stimuli, deprivations, and reinforcers appear to control his speech, and give a "plausible reconstruction" of how a past history of reinforcement has created this control.

Notice that in this case we are starting with an accomplished speaker. This is because engineering learning to talk and maintaining talking throughout a lifetime are two different reinforcement scheduling problems, and hence require somewhat different analyses. Our emphasis will remain on the speaker's behavior, not on his words or "what he means to say." There are several reasons for ignoring words, as such, right now. A word is a response by the speaker but is a stimulus to the hearer. Saying words is caused by different things than hearing words; one doesn't simply run the language-generating machinery in reverse gear when one is listening. But concentrating our attention on words as such would tend to cause us to bypass these important issues; hence our dismissal of the problems of words and meanings for the present.

We are restricting ourselves to an account of *vocal verbal behavior*, that is, talking. There is *non*verbal vocal behavior:

Snoring
Gasping
Making sounds such as "ooff" or "aaagh"
Whistling
Humming tunes

The last two are operant, as you can see when someone is calling a taxi, whistling "Dixie," or *showing* you how the melody goes. The others are not operant because they do not depend upon a past history of reinforcement for their existence. They are not conditioned the way the last two are.

There is nonvocal verbal behavior:

Writing—it has a different vocabulary, rate, set of controlling stimuli, set of reinforcers—just about everything
Gesture
Facial expression
Typing
Typesetting
The special "languages" of flowers, gems, and stamps
Telegraphy

All of these are interesting and worthy of further study, but they are not germane to our main purpose here.

THE WRONG PARADIGM

It is unlikely that anyone other than the Pavlovian psychologists of the Soviet Union now talks about verbal behavior in the following way, but some people used to be taught the "wrong paradigm" for verbal behavior in their psychology courses. We now know that verbal behavior is operant behavior, but at one time, when operant behavior was not well understood, verbal behavior was said to be acquired by the process illustrated in the following paradigm.

$$\begin{array}{c} \text{CS} \\ + \\ \text{US} \longrightarrow \text{UR} \end{array} \qquad \text{LATER} \quad \text{CS} \longrightarrow \text{CR}$$

As you know, this is called Pavlovian or classical or respondent conditioning. It consists of the pairing of some stimulus that doesn't elicit a reflex response (the CS) with one that does (the US). After a number of such pairings, sometimes as few as one, a response, the conditioned response (CR), which is the same as or similar to the unconditioned response (UR), will come to be elicited by the presentation of the CS alone. In Pavlov's classical example, the US was meat and the CS was the ringing of a bell. The UR elicited by the US was salivation, and the pairing of the bell (CS) and food (US) was sufficient to establish a CR of salivation to the CS (bell) alone.

When the Pavlovian paradigm is applied to the verbal behavior situation, something like what is depicted in the following illustration is supposed to happen.

FIRST:

(PET)

+

"DOG"   "DOG"
(VOICE OF ADULT)   (VOICE OF CHILD)

LATER

"DOG"
(VOICE OF CHILD)

It was claimed that the child learns to say "dog" when he sees the animal, because the sight of the animal is paired with the sound of the adult saying "dog." That is, the voice of the adult saying "dog" is a US which elicits the child's UR of saying "dog," and the mere pairing of the CS, the sight of the dog, with the US will cause the child to later emit the CR "dog" to the CS, the sight of the dog. Well, you can see where following that road would take us. The Pavlovian view of verbal behavior suggests several very dubious notions.

One.   It was said, at one time, that *dog* "is a sign for," "symbolizes," "signals," "stands for," or "represents" the missing animal. That is, it was said that we respond to the name as we would respond to the thing. That point of view runs into severe problems, for we neither feed nor pet the sound, nor does it scratch us or make us sneeze. This problem is not limited to dogs, for we do not respond to the sound as if it were the thing itself when someone says "skunk," "ice," "bee," "unicorn," "square root of two," "red," "bed," "free beer," or "orange."

Two. The Pavlovian paradigm requires that the adult's verbal response (I use the symbol Rv for a verbal response) function as a stimulus (I add another symbol to indicate the stimulus function of a verbal response, that is, Rv:S) and *elicit* the Rv "dog." It is claimed that we learn to "name" this way. The *illicit* term in the Pavlovian account is *elicit.* "Dog" can serve either as a Rv or as a discriminative stimulus, but it is not an eliciting stimulus (US or CS) for talking. The Pavlovian paradigm is not applicable here because verbal behavior is not elicited behavior. It is not made up of the responses of reflexes (US-UR relationships). There are no real, identifiable, empirical, biologically determined unconditioned eliciting stimuli (US's) for talking. Hence, it will be wiser for us to ignore the Pavlovian approach and use the operant conditioning paradigm instead.

INTERLOCKING PARADIGM

We may now look at what Skinner has called the *interlocking verbal behavior paradigm.* This allows us to see in a most general and simplified way how the variables (S^D, Dep'n, Rv, S^R) arrange themselves in a verbal episode. The justification of the claim that the items in the real world are functioning in the way that we say they do is most general and sketchy at this point. This is a promissory note of sorts. Much more will come later; I'll pay off this intellectual debt and tighten things up. But, let us look at the next illustration to begin.

```
FIRST
A: "MAY I HAVE A HOT DOG"
B:

NEXT
A:
B: "CERTAINLY" (HANDS ONE TO A)

NEXT
A: "THANKS" (TAKES HOT DOG AND BITES)
B:

NEXT
A:
B: "ANY TIME"
```

It's not great literature, but you might well hear something like it in a film of the realist style, because it is verbal behavior. No ideas, information, or symbols are displayed, but nonetheless it is verbal behavior.

Our problem here is to apply the simple operant paradigm shown on page 8 to each response displayed in the preceding illustration. To do this, we must look for instances of controlling circumstances, that is, discriminative stimuli and deprivations. The next illustration identifies the relevant Rv's and discriminative stimuli for the interchange depicted in the preceding illustration. Notice that the double-tailed arrows indicate that an event that has one function for the person who emits it may have a different functional property for the person who receives it. For example, A's "Thanks" is a Rv for A, but a discriminative stimulus for B.

A: S^D ⟶ Rv "MAY I HAVE A HOT DOG" S^D ⟶ R TAKES Rv "THANKS"

DEP^N +   + $S^D_{HOT\ DOG}$

B: ⟶ Rv "CERTAINLY" S^D ⟶ Rv "ANY TIME"
        S^D ⟶ R GIVES

We notice that each response is caused by some preceding occurrence; nothing just happens by itself, all of a sudden. It starts with A's food deprivation ("hunger") and the presence of B, who is an *audience*. Lacking the discriminative stimulus of an audience, A would have to do something else. He might go home and make a snack, or go down the hall and put a dime in the vending machine. But these wouldn't be verbal behaviors.

Next, we must find the reinforcers. The next illustration is the same as the preceding one with the exception of the identification of the reinforcing stimuli as such.

A: S^D ⟶ Rv "MAY I HAVE A HOT DOG" ⟶ $S^{r \cdot D}$ ⟶ R TAKES / Rv "THANKS" ⟶ S^r

DEP^N

B: S^D ⟹ R GIVES / R "CERTAINLY" ⟶ $S^{r \cdot D}$ ⟶ Rv "ANY TIME"

Determining which events are reinforcers will help us evaluate the significance of this interaction for the future behavior of the two speakers. Notice that an event can be both a discriminative stimulus and a reinforcer for the same speaker (I use the symbol $S^{r \cdot D}$). The assertion that these things are properly called reinforcers may be supported at several levels of definiteness and precision. Let's again do it loosely now.

Remember that reinforcement increases the probability of the recurrence of the preceding response in the presence of its controlling circumstances. That the items identified as reinforcers in the preceding illustration are reinforcers seems quite obvious. How they got that way is another story. You know part of it already, and I will supply the rest later. So, clearly, the hot dog is a reinforcer. A person who never got one this way would not be likely to keep on asking. "Thanks" is also a reinforcer. It is somewhat harder to see why, and this is the loose part of the explanation which will have to be tightened up later. A's saying "Thanks" tends to be correlated with other reinforcing behavior on his part. It is functionally a promise to do something for B some other time—for example, passing the butter, buying him a doughnut, lending him his car—when B is the one who will get the obvious reinforcer and will probably be the first speaker. B seems to find the "Thanks" reinforcing. If such behavior is omitted, B may complain about what a chiseler A is, even to the extent of verbally or manually attacking him. That is, we see that *aversive stimulation* may be provided by B if A doesn't emit the appropriate reinforcer. Furthermore, if A emits the Rv, but won't take the opposite role later (i.e., doesn't follow through), B *discounts* A's gratitude and may behave just as if A had never emitted the Rv "Thanks."

"Any time" reinforces A's emission of the Rv "Thanks" by registering B's disposition to go through this episode or similar ones in the future.

A justification for claiming that these stimuli are reinforcing will have to be developed in detail later. But, for the present we can see that they do not depart in any important way from the general descriptions of reinforcers to which we are accustomed. Importantly, they are real, observable stimuli, and they occur where they should if they are to perform the reinforcer's role.

This whole business occurs without any special intent or awareness on the part of the participants. No one is sitting there calculating. No one says, "I'll reinforce you, if you will reinforce me." Often, if asked, the participants are completely unaware of the contingencies and the stimulus functions. It is not necessary to know a behavioral or a physical law in order to be governed by it. If one's behavior is describable by a set of rules, it does not imply that one knows the rules in any significant sense. Since time immemorial humans have been pressed down upon the surface of the earth by a force. Their behavior of not leaving the earth is governed by the rule $F = m_M \cdot m_E \cdot G / r^2$; Where m_M is the mass of the man, m_E is the mass of the earth, r is the earth's radius, and G is the universal constant of gravitation, while F is the magnitude of the force pressing the man to the surface of the earth. Until Newton discovered this rule, no one knew it, but everyone followed it. My liver follows rules in converting glucose (sugar) into glycogen, but I don't know them in any ordinary sense of the word *know*. If it is claimed that in some special sense I do, then it must be claimed that my liver knows not only chemistry but algebra, calculus, and quantum physics. It then seems to me that saying that there exists some special *knowing* of this sort is just using the word in such a peculiar way so as to turn the whole discussion into a debate about the meanings of words, rather than an inquiry into what people can or cannot do.

A retraction of sorts (not really): Our example is not absolutely general. It is a nice easy one, and thus a good place to begin. And, it has that one, good, obvious reinforcer, the hot dog. Some examples are harder:

A: How are you today, sir?
B: Fine, thanks.

We will have to get through several chapters before we have discussed enough of the analysis so that we can handle that one.

Here are some implications of the interlocking verbal paradigm. They don't sound like what we have been considering thus far, but they follow from it.

Verbal behavior is social behavior. Skinner has defined SOCIAL BEHAVIOR AS THAT BEHAVIOR WHOSE REINFORCEMENT IS MEDIATED BY AN-OTHER ORGANISM. Of course, most of what social psychologists study is also social behavior in this sense. But a lot of other things are also social behavior in this sense, including verbal behavior. The contingency (the arrow), between the Rv and the reinforcer is always maintained by another organism. The other animal may be a pet dog or cat, but there must be another organism. That's because nature or machinery does not reinforce verbal behavior. Oranges don't jump off the tree into your mouth when you say "Please" or "I'm hungry." Never mind about the yodeler who starts avalanches by warbling, or the opera singer who cracks hotel windows as fast as terrorist bombs. First of all, it's not very important. Second, and more important, although these are vocal behaviors, they are not vocal verbal behaviors.

In verbal behavior, as in all cases of social behavior, a person can increase the likelihood that he will get reinforced. He does this simply by reinforcing the behavior of the REINFORCEMENT MEDIATOR (THE FELLOW WHO ACTS AS A REINFORCER DISPENSER) which produces reinforcements for himself. If I have apples and you have bananas, and bananas are reinforcing to me at the moment but apples are not, and, if apples are reinforcing to you, then I can reinforce you for reinforcing me. I simply give you an apple each time you give me a banana. Sounds like Economics I, doesn't it? The sociologist and social psychologist George Homans thought so and has written a very good book about it.

But what about the "Thanks" and the "Any time"? They are not the same as the bananas of the fruit exchange of the immediately preceding example. Remember that these are *conditioned reinforcers*, and, as we will see later, they have the additional functional role of setting things up for the future. Each speaker, by dispensing such conditioned reinforcers, increases the probability that the other will comply in some future exchange.

Even if the reinforcers work, an important feature of social behavior is that reinforcement mediators are not perfectly reliable. The hearer may or may not have any coffee, cigarettes, milk, beer, cars, or money. People are less reliable than machines. (Come now, you know that is true. How many times has what's his name who sits next to you in class been out of cigarettes or candy bars or sticks of gum when you wanted one, and how many times has the machine been out or not worked? Have you really counted?) So, verbal behavior, like all social behavior, is intermittently reinforced. And, like all intermittently reinforced behavior, it becomes very persistent. If reinforcements aren't immediately forthcoming, the behavior continues on and on (the nagging wife). When the machine is the reinforcement mediator, if reinforcements are not delivered, emotional behavior ensues; people kick it, hit it, scream at it. They behave just like the rat who is EX-TINGUISHED (NOT REINFORCED) AFTER HAVING BEEN CONTINUOUSLY REIN-FORCED (REINFORCED EACH TIME).

SIZE OF UNITS OF ANALYSIS

A problem which I have been avoiding ought now to be squarely faced. To make this sort of analysis work, we have to isolate single events or items in verbal behavior. We have to determine units of analysis. We have to decide when something has happened. The pigeon's peck is easy. It has a discrete unity, and it recycles and repeats. But listen to "May I have a hot dog" when you say it to yourself. It flows—there are no stops or discrete units, there is no recycling, there aren't any pauses or blank spaces. It seems to be just a stream. Spoken speech has no pauses between words or double spaces after colons. What then is the utterance? Is it one thing, an intact sentence? Is it six things, words? Is it a whole lot of things, phones (speech sounds)? Here is the gist of the answer to these sorts of questions. Distinguish between the response (Rv) and the verbal operant. Rv's exist at many levels of complexity; we will examine some. Operants are functional units, unambiguous and unequivocal. We'll see as follows.

We can begin by concentrating on responses and looking at several of the possible ways of decomposing any utterance (Rv) into its parts. If we take into account only the structural properties of verbal behavior, we will find that the work has already been done. This was originally taken to be the province of structural linguistics (another discipline concerned with verbal behavior). By using the methods of paired comparisons, linguists identified PHONEMES, THE MINIMAL SOUNDS OR COMBINATIONS OF SOUNDS THAT ARE PERCEIVED AS BEING DIFFERENT IN A GIVEN SPEECH COMMUNITY. The difference between the *b* sound and the *p* sound in "bit" and "pit" and in "bin" and "pin" constitutes one phonemic difference, while the difference between the *i* sound and the *e* sound in "pin" and "pen" constitutes another, according to Bloomfield.

Phonemes are not letters. It is claimed that you need somewhere between twenty-eight (Jakobson, Fant, and Halle) and forty-nine (Bloomfield) phonemes to completely describe spoken English in its Received American, sometimes called Chicago Standard, version, whereas the twenty-six letters of the written alphabet suffice for transcription. The international phonetic "alphabet" has about fifty symbols which are claimed to be sufficient to represent all the sounds that are discriminated as different in all the languages spoken today. Again, there are differences of opinion on this. Bloomfield claimed that no spoken language had fewer than fifteen phonemes nor did any have more than fifty, whereas Kagan and Haveman claim that the number of phonemes for spoken languages varies from fifteen to eighty and that Received American English has forty-five.

Furthermore, different communities "carve up" the speech spectrum into different phonemes. They do not make the same discriminations. The vowel sounds in "pin" and "pen" are very different to people who live in the New York City or Chicago areas, but sound the same to people who live in central and western Texas. For the Texans, there is one phoneme, but the New Yorkers hear two. Similarly, according to Bloomfield, speakers of Menomeni (a Native American language) say that the following sound the same: "bad" and "bat," also "swede" and "sweet." What are two phonemes for us are one for them.

MORPHEMES ARE MINIMAL SPEECH INTERVALS WHICH ARE DISCRIMINATED AS HAVING MEANING. "A" is both a morpheme and a phoneme. All the one-syllable words are morphemes, although each is generally composed of several phonemes. Roots and affixes are morphemes, for example, "manu," "ped," "un," "ite," "s," "ings," "ly."

Words, curiously, are probably not structurally speech units. The word seems to have resisted linguistic definition. No structural property of spoken speech seems capable of being used to identify words, not even pausing. We do not pause after each word when we speak; listen to a tape recording some time and concentrate on how things are said rather than what is said. Although the word does not seem to be a natural unit, it seems to have been, and to still be, a useful concept. Bloomfield wrote: "The word is not primarily a phonetic unit: we do not, by pauses or other phonetic features mark off those segments of our speech which could be spoken alone." However, "the analysis of linguistic forms into words is familiar to us because we have the custom of leaving spaces between words in our writing and printing. People who have not learned to read and write, have some difficulty when, by any chance, they are called upon to make word divisions. This difficulty is less in English than in some other languages, such as French." George Miller said that the custom of dividing written material into separate words arose with the invention of printing. The Greek and Roman writers left no blank spaces between words. Thus, the word seems to be a printer's convention which has been generally adopted by literate people.

Sentences might be defined as grammatically intact, received (acceptable) utterances. Almost no one talks in grammatical sentences all the time. The rather unusual people who do are said to "talk like a book." If you, make an absolutely literal transcription of what the president says when giving his news conference (not reading his prepared statement), or what the professor says when giving his lecture, and then turn it in as an English I composition, you will get back all sorts of scribbles in red pencil about "run-ons" and "fragments."

Therefore, the structure of speech alone tells us nothing about the location or sizes of its component parts, except that they might exist at any of several levels of complexity. The question remains, "which one shall we choose to use, and why should we choose, at that?"

Let us recall that our purpose is to analyze verbal behavior in terms of its controlling variables. If we arbitrarily select some unit of analysis, we will be prejudging the issue of at what level controlling variables act. That is, if we select some particular level of analysis, we will admit or discover only the variables that operate at that level. But, as we will see, different variables operate at different levels. We can see the correctness of this sort of reasoning by looking at some examples of the effects of variables at different levels of the linguistic hierarchy.

Phoneme: Normal nonliterary verbal behavior shows that some causes operate to produce verbal behavior at the phoneme level of simplicity. If such causes persist, the behavior persists, and the same phonemes tend to recur. Thus, ordinary speech tends to have rhyme and alliteration "without intent" on the part of the speaker. Here are two examples taken from remarks made by members of the House of Representatives' Committee on the Judiciary during hearings on the impeachment of Richard M. Nixon: "A *text* torn out of con*text* is a pre*text*." "If we are to have *c*onfidence in the *c*oncept of equal treatment under the law, we *c*annot *c*ondone this *k*ind of *c*onduct."

Word: Other causes seem to produce responses at the level of words. In the following examples, let me present the cause, and you do the responding:

> Questions sometimes operate at this level—
> Who wrote the Gettysburg Address?
> Who is the president of the United States?
> What is the capital of France?
> But other variables, not questions, do too—
> As wise as an . . .
> He invented the electric light bulb.
> Father Christmas
> Mama Bear, Papa Bear, and Baby . . .

Phrase: These are easy; again, I'll supply a controlling variable and notice how your responses are multiword phrases:

> Snow White and the . . .
> A penny saved is a . . .
> He who hesitates . . .
> Honi soit qui mal . . .

That last one isn't an effective variable for the same kind of verbal behavior as the others, unless you have had some special past history of reinforcement called French lessons.

Big ones: Some causal variables are peculiar. The class bell produces fifty minutes of talking by me. There are some people for whom "Do you know the Gettysburg Address?" is a causal variable such that they say: "Fourscore and seven years ago . . ." and don't pause or stop until " . . . and that government of the people, by the people, for the people, shall not perish from the earth." One's audience has certain controlling effects. The vocabulary I use in my classes is quite different, as is my speed of talking, from that occurring when I discuss the same subject matter with the other professors at the lunch table. The language the minister uses in the church service is very different from that used in his bedroom, even though the issues under discussion may be the same.

We may conclude, then, that since causal analysis is our goal, we cannot fix the size of the response unit; we must let it vary from small to large. It will change from the smallest and simplest unit to the largest and most complex, depending upon the controlling variables present. This leaves us free to discover which variables are operating at all levels, since they exist at all levels. This lets the data decide. Put another way, the size of the unit of the dependent variable for verbal behavior is not a structural question; it is a functional one.

This all tells us that the appropriate unit is not simply a response but a functional unit, a cause-effect relationship, namely, the *verbal operant.*

A *verbal operant* is merely a disposition (tendency, likelihood) to respond in a certain way to a certain state of affairs because of a past history of reinforcement. This is just like our nonverbal example of the pigeon's key-peck. Look at the first illustration in Chapter 1 again. Remember that an operant has three components: (1) antecedent causal variables (deprivation or discriminative stimuli), (2) a response, and (3) a controlling relationship between the first and the second (the arrow). The members of each "end" of an operant are classes, and a certain amount of variability is permitted among members of the antecedent or the response class. So, variability in size, color, fur, and so on, occurs among the discriminative stimuli (animals) for the Rv "dog." But if one discriminative stimulus is an animal, and another is printing or writing on paper, we have the situation depicted in the following illustration. Here we have *two* operants, with only one Rv, which is shared by both of them.

We can have some, but not much, variation on the response side. If the response varies a great deal, as in the three cases depicted in the next illustration, we get into several different operants (three shown in the illustration) under the control of the same causal variable. Each operant in these last two illustrations has a different reinforcement history; each is a different tendency to respond and has a different strength.

Although the antecedents (deprivation or discriminative stimuli) and the consequent Rv of an operant can vary, their variation within a given operant is not great, and any changes in them tend to occur slowly. Therefore, what varies principally in operants, and over a wide range with surprising rapidity, is the strength of the disposition (tendency) to respond. That is, what changes is the likelihood of the Rv *given* the controlling variable. This likelihood (probability) can vary from 0 to 1. It exists due to a past history of reinforcement and varies (is greater or lesser) depending upon the number, size, quality, and schedule of reinforcements that have been obtained in the past. If a response has been reinforced in the presence of a discriminative stimulus many times in the past, its probability of recurrence (strength of the operant) will be close to 1. For example, consider the discriminative stimulus "What is your name?" If the response has occurred only rarely in the presence of the discriminative stimulus, and hence has been reinforced only rarely, the strength may be close to 0. Consider the discriminative stimulus "What was Mrs. Washington's maiden name?"

INDICES OF OPERANT STRENGTH

Skinner argues that the verbal operant is what we need, what we want to know about. If we knew a speaker's past history of reinforcement, we would know his verbal operants, and *when* he would speak and *what* he would say, and relatively how likely he would be to say it in those circumstances. In principle the past history of reinforcement is knowable; in practice it isn't feasible. That is, in principle we could follow a person all the time and record everything that happened to him since his birth, but in practice we haven't the resources. In practice, it is hard to measure the probability of a Rv in a given set of circumstances. Rate of repetition, the dependent variable for the pigeon, won't do. We are shaped by our reinforcing communities to speak only once. The first time is interesting; the second and third times are boring, and punishment ensues.

In practice, then, the best that we can do is to present a suspected controlling variable, and record the resulting verbal behavior, if there is any. Whatever gets said is the Rv of the strongest operant having that controlling variable. There are a number of ways to do this. The *word association* test gives us the most probable Rv when the discriminative stimulus is a spoken or written word. The *opposites* test and the various *vocabulary* tests give us similar data with different sorts of discriminative stimuli. By using a tachistoscope, we can present written words briefly, and measure probability by counting the frequency of brief exposures required before a Rv is given. Or else we can progressively lengthen the exposure time, and measure probability by the reciprocal of the time elapsed before a Rv occurs.

Above all, there is no intensive property of the Rv alone, except its occurrence, that is a reliable indicator of operant strength. We might have supposed that some property of the Rv itself would tell, but the following examples show that the desirable degree of reliability is far from present.

Repetition: "No, no, a thousand times no" seems stronger than "Well, no-o." But, a Rv emitted just once is not necessarily weak: "Please dear, just this once," or "I am delighted to accept the nomination to be your candidate for president," or "Take the money; just don't shoot me."

Loudness: Strong reflexes have large response magnitudes, and a screamed Rv may be part of a strong operant. But, one does not shout his name when introduced. "Sweet nothings" are usually whispered, but may be very strongly determined. Prisoners plotting an escape do not yell their plans to the guards. Mothers, when visiting the library with their children, hiss instructions to be quiet.

Rapidity: (This is not the same as rate. RATE IS THE FREQUENCY OF REPETITION OF A RESPONSE PER UNIT TIME; RAPIDITY IS THE RECIPROCAL OF THE DURATION OF THE RESPONSE, I.E., HOW FAST EACH RESPONSE IS.) Bad news is delivered, unavoidably, but often in a halting manner.

Combining all these points into one grotesque example, we see that even though his behavior is strongly determined, the policeman speaks quietly and slowly, rather than running up screaming at two hundred words a minute: "YOUR WIFE IS DEAD; YOUR HOUSE AND KIDS ARE ALL BURNT UP; ALL BURNT UP, ALL, ALL; EVERY ONE, EVERY-THING; ALL BURNT UP, ALL BURNT UP; ALL, ALL, ALL; DEAD, DEAD, DEAD."

REPETITION, LOUDNESS, AND RAPIDITY ARE ALL PRODUC-TION EFFECTS, USUALLY. The operants give the speaker "something to say." If the controlling relation between the antecedent and the Rv is strong, it will be said. But separate variables which act in a "supple-mentary" way determine the special production effects. All these aspects of speaking are caused, but by different things. We will discuss this in much more detail later.

Skinner's invention of the cumulative recorder made recording the occurrence of the pigeon's key-peck and what preceded and followed it very easy. In recording verbal behavior, we have to decide what terms are to be used in the description of the events that we intend to explain. Here precision and fidelity, which, thanks to technology, are easily come by, may be mistaken for "more scientific." Recording can be as detailed as you like. We can reproduce the acoustic effects with almost complete fidelity by using magnetic tape recording. We can make records of which muscles move by the process called electromyography. We can make a phonetic transcription, using the international phonetic alphabet or one of its equivalents. We can write down direct quotations ("You, sir, are a rascal"), as the court reporter does. Or we can use indirect quotation (He said that Jones was a bad person), which would be a "written description of the import of the speaker's utterance."

Direct quotation is sufficient for our purposes. It names the behavior emitted and describes it, because the name actually resembles the thing named (perhaps this is the only case in which it does). Indirect quotation is too far from specifying behavior. A speaker whose behavior is indirectly quoted may have spoken in another language, or gestured, or used "different words." The other methods of recording generally provide more detail than we need.

Describing the antecedents, causal variables, in operants is less of a problem. The causal variables are only deprivations, aversive stimulation, and various sorts of discriminative stimuli. But they fall into a number of subclasses which depend upon different kinds of reinforcement contingencies. We will look at how each of these antecedents affects Rv's, and how, in terms of past histories of reinforcement, it got control. To use Skinner's terminology, we will look at

Deprivation and aversive stimulation as parts of *mands*;

Discriminative stimuli for *tacts*;

The *audience* as a discriminative stimulus;

Discriminative stimuli for *textuals*;

Discriminative stimuli for *echoic* behavior;

Discriminative stimuli for *intraverbals*; and, finally,

Multiple causation and *autoclitic behavior*, or how the variables converge to produce "real speech."

3

mands

Because deprivation and aversive stimulation differ from the other types of controlling variables for verbal operants (which are discriminative stimuli of one sort or another), it is wise to look at them separately. So, in this chapter we will look at deprivation and aversive stimulation (S^{AV}) and the mand as a class of verbal operants. We may begin with a definition.

DEFINITION AND PARADIGM

A MAND IS A VERBAL OPERANT WHOSE CONTROLLING VARIABLE IS A DEPRIVATION OR AN AVERSIVE STIMULUS, AND WHOSE R$_V$ SPECIFIES ITS RE-INFORCER. "Specifies" here does not imply meaning in any metaphysical way. "Specifies" here is equivalent to "is the conventional name of," but, more precisely, according to Chapter 4, "specifies its reinforcer" is equivalent to "would tact its reinforcer, if the reinforcer were present."

The word *mand* is a *neologism* (i.e., a new word made up for the occasion) and is related to such words as command, demand, and mandatory. *Mand, tact, autoclitic, echoic, intraverbal,* and *textual* are all neologisms that Skinner made up and used in his book *Verbal Behavior*. But, and we should be perfectly clear on this, our use of such terms in this book differs somewhat from Skinner's.

Our definition of *mand* includes "specifies its reinforcer." This means that the Rv of a mand tells the reinforcement mediator (the individual who functions like the pigeon's food dispenser and gives the speaker the reinforcer) exactly what he must do to reinforce the mand. Reinforcement mediators are, by virtue of being members of a verbal community, conditioned to respond to some Rv's in highly specific (conventional) ways which are reinforcing to the speaker. The next illustration shows a paradigm of the interaction between the speaker and the reinforcement mediator in the case of mands. In this instance there is a characteristic conventional covariation between the form of the Rv and the form of the R that the mediator emits.

$$
\begin{array}{l}
\text{SPEAKER} \quad \begin{array}{c} S^{AV} \\ \text{OR} \\ \text{DEP}^{\underline{N}} \end{array} \longrightarrow \text{Rv} \longrightarrow S^{R} \\[2mm]
\hline \\
\text{REINFORCEMENT} \\
\text{MEDIATOR} \qquad\qquad S^{D} \longrightarrow R
\end{array}
$$

Our definition asserts that whenever this is true, the controlling variable for the Rv will be either a deprivation or an aversive stimulus.

Let us look at some simple examples. The following could be mands. But, beware! We never know from observing the Rv *alone* what the controlling variable is. No Rv itself, or any of its intensive properties, is diagnostic of its controlling variables. We will go into this in detail after a few pages, but now the examples:

Response	Reinforcer
"May I have a hot dog"	Hot dog
"Iced tea, please"	Iced tea
"Waiter"	Waiter comes
"Quit it"	Annoyance stops
"Put away your rubbers"	Rubbers gone
"Chase your tail"	Dog runs in circles
"Get off my foot"	Gets off

If you know what the reinforcer was, you know what the reinforcement mediator did. And, within broad limits, if you know what the reinforcer is, you know what the mand term for it is. Thus the reinforcement mediator who hears these Rv forms *may* reinforce. If he does, he makes a different response in each case. Hence, the speaker's Rv specifies the reinforcement; the reinforcement characteristics covary with the Rv.

WHY DEPRIVATION AND AVERSIVE
STIMULATION BECOME CONTROLLING

This may, at first, seem mysterious because normally the reinforcement mediator doesn't stop to find out if an appropriate state of deprivation exists or if an aversive stimulus is affecting the speaker. He makes his "complying response" solely on the basis of the speaker's Rv, as shown in the paradigm for the mand. The reinforcement mediator may not comply on a given occasion, but that doesn't destroy the relationship. For when he does, he is usually indifferent to or unaware of the state of the speaker. One of the occasional exceptions occurs when the speaker is a child who says, "Hot dog, please." His mother may interject, "He's not hungry."

So, how does the appropriate antecedent condition get control? The answer has two parts which are related, but a digression on the nature of reinforcers must come between the two parts.

Reinforcers specified by mands may be of two sorts: One sort depends on deprivation for its momentary effectiveness; the other sort depends on the presence of an aversive stimulus for its momentary effectiveness. Dependence on deprivation is true of some positive unconditioned reinforcers (what we denote by S^R). The next illustration shows two prototypes. In both of these cases the speaker must be deprived or else the unconditioned reinforcer will not work, that is, reinforcement doesn't occur even if the reinforcing stimulus is presented to the speaker. He won't engage in consummatory behavior (eating or drinking) unless deprived, and he does so only if deprived. And, the mediator's behavior is reinforcing to the speaker only if the latter engages in consummatory behavior thereafter. Furthermore, the occurrence of that deprivation will, in the future, increase the probability of the emission of that Rv. This is what Skinner and I mean by "controlling behavior."

$$\text{SPEAKER:} \quad \text{Rv} \begin{array}{c} \text{"MAY I HAVE} \\ \text{A DRINK"} \end{array} \longrightarrow S^R \text{ ALCOHOL}$$
$$+$$
$$\text{DEP}^N$$

$$\text{SPEAKER:} \quad \text{Rv "POPCORN PLEASE"} \longrightarrow S^R \text{ POPCORN}$$
$$+$$
$$\text{DEP}^N$$

REMINDER OF HOW REINFORCERS WORK

We have to embark on a digression about reinforcers, especially their classification and mechanism of operation. Some people seem to be still quite confused about this. We may divide this discussion in two, dealing, respectively, with (1) the positive and (2) the negative reinforcers.

Deprivation is important for some positive reinforcers. If these stimuli are withheld from an organism, their effectiveness increases. THE UNCONDITIONED POSITIVE REINFORCERS (S^R's) ARE SPECIES SPECIFIC. They form a very short list; for example, food, water, air, rest, activity. The upper part of the next illustration depicts a typical nonverbal example (a rat in a box with a chain to pull and a bar to press). The reinforcing effect of food depends upon the rat's being deprived of food, and with the consumption of the food the reinforcement is completed. Some simple examples involving Rv's were given in the illustration before the last.

$$\text{DEP}^N \begin{cases} S^{D}\ \text{LIGHT} \longrightarrow R\ ^{\text{CHAIN}}_{\text{PULL}} \longrightarrow S^{R}\ \text{FOOD} \\[2ex] S^{D}\ \text{DARK} \longrightarrow R\ ^{\text{BAR-}}_{\text{PRESS}} \longrightarrow S^{r \cdot D}\ \text{LIGHT} \longrightarrow R\ ^{\text{CHAIN}}_{\text{PULL}} \longrightarrow S^{R}\ \text{FOOD} \end{cases}$$

ANY STIMULUS THAT IS TEMPORALLY AND SPATIALLY PAIRED WITH OR A MEANS TO AN UNCONDITIONED REINFORCER BECOMES A CONDITIONED REINFORCER (S^r). Deprivation for the unconditioned reinforcer to which it has been a means, maximizes the reinforcing effectiveness of the conditioned reinforcer. The list of conditioned reinforcers for any given animal tends to be long and idiosyncratic. The lower part of the preceding illustration gives a typical nonverbal example of conditioned reinforcement using the rat in the box with the chain and bar. The probability of the rat's pressing the bar goes up only if he is deprived of food; light deprivation won't do it. We may notice that the light is both a reinforcing stimulus and a discriminative stimulus for the rat. Since one thing does both jobs, we may denote it with the symbol $S^{r \cdot D}$. The next illustration shows a complex case involving both the verbal and the nonverbal behavior of a hungry person. Again, stimuli may act as both reinforcers and discriminative stimuli—reinforcing those behaviors that preceded them and serving as discriminative stimuli for the responses that follow them. Notice that deprivation is relatively constant here. One deprivation is present throughout the entire episode. It makes many conditioned reinforcers effective and therefore controls many mands, although only one mand is unconditionally reinforced.

AVERSIVE STIMULI (S^{Av}) ARE NEGATIVE REINFORCERS. THEY STILL REINFORCE, THAT IS, THEY INCREASE THE PROBABILITY OF THE RESPONSE IN THE PRESENCE OF THE ANTECEDENT CONDITIONS. HOWEVER, THESE REINFORCERS DO SO BY BEING TERMINATED (TURNED OFF). THERE ARE BOTH CONDI-

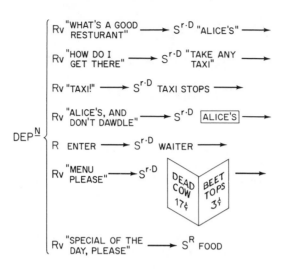

TIONED (S^{r-}) AND UNCONDITIONED (S^{R-}) NEGATIVE REINFORCERS. THE NEGA-TIVE ONES, AS IN THE POSITIVE REINFORCER CASE, ARE BIOLOGICALLY GIVEN AND DO NOT DEPEND ON A PAST HISTORY OF PAIRING FOR THEIR EFFECTIVE-NESS. The next illustration depicts a typical nonverbal example of negative reinforcement. (The shock comes on every once in a while and stays on until the rat presses the bar, whereupon it goes off and stays off for a while. This produces a high probability of bar-pressing when the shock appears. Thus, the shock is both a negative reinforcer and a discriminative stimulus. We may therefore denote both functions as follows: $S^{R-\cdot D}$; and if the reinforcer is a conditioned negative one, we denote its reinforcing and discriminative stimulus functions as $S^{r-\cdot D}$.)

Notice that it is mechanically impossible to use a negative reinforcer when the animal is not appropriately aversively stimulated. The stimulus must be present before it is terminated.

$$S^{R-\cdot D} \text{ SHOCK ON} \longrightarrow R \text{ PRESS BAR} \longrightarrow S^{R-} \text{ SHOCK OFF} \longrightarrow Pr(R \mid S^{R-\cdot D})\uparrow$$

The next illustration gives some examples of negative reinforcement involving Rv's and both conditioned and unconditioned negative reinforcers. Here the controlling relation is very visible because a "public" stimulus is present.

$S^{R-\cdot D}$ FAT MAN ON FOOT $\longrightarrow$ Rv "GET OFF MY FOOT" $\longrightarrow$ S^{R-} TERMINATES

$S^{R-\cdot D}$ TWIST EAR $\longrightarrow$ Rv "I GIVE UP" $\longrightarrow$ S^{R-} TERMINATES

$S^{R-\cdot D}$ RAIN $\longrightarrow$ Rv "OPEN THE UMBRELLA" $\longrightarrow$ S^{R-} TERMINATES

$S^{r-\cdot D}$ STICK OUT TONGUE $\longrightarrow$ Rv "STOP IT" $\longrightarrow$ S^{r-} TERMINATES

$S^{r-\cdot D}$ SIGHT OF HYPODERMIC SYRINGE $\longrightarrow$ Rv "NO, NO, NO" $\longrightarrow$ S^{r-} TERMINATES

$S^{r-\cdot D}$ RUBBERS ON FLOOR $\longrightarrow$ Rv "PUT AWAY YOUR RUBBERS" $\longrightarrow$ S^{r-} TERMINATES

We may thus conclude the first part of our answer to the question of how deprivation and aversive stimulation get control as follows. They do so *without* the mediator's arranging for them to do so. He doesn't have to worry about it. If the mediator attempts to reinforce at any other time, it doesn't work. Such other times get no control. We may say that the laws of psychology take care of it. Either deprivation or aversive stimulation must be present for the attempted reinforcement operation to work. And, anything routinely present at the time of reinforcement gets control over the response.

Now, here is a peculiarity of mands, and the second part of the answer. *Nothing else is routinely present.* Deprivation and aversive stimulation have essentially no competition from environmental (discriminative stimulus) control. The next illustration helps us compare mands with nonverbal deprivation dependent behavior. The Rv "May I have a hot dog" does not covary with the environment. You can do it upstairs, downstairs, in the swimming pool, inside, outside, and even upside down in an airplane. There may or may not be a hot dog in view. The mand works in a wide variety of situations. Verbal behavior is very free; the speaker can speak at any time and needs no special environmental props. Even though an auditor is likely to be present when speech occurs, his characteristics do not determine which Rv will be emitted. Nor does the Rv or mand that occurs reveal anything about the speaker's external environment; it doesn't vary with it. How unlike the nonverbal alternative to the mand this is. The hot dog in the refrigerator governs the probability, the location in space and time, and the form of the response to it. By contrast, in the purest case of the mand there is absolutely no outside influence, such as in the isolated desert-dwelling hermit's cry, "Water."

Let me issue a warning. Don't be tempted to argue that mands are *in fact* secretly controlled by stimuli arising from the absence of the item. That is, don't try to claim that the discriminative stimulus of no hot dog controls the Rv "hot dog." If you were to make such a claim, you would put yourself

NONVERBAL CASE

$$\text{DEP}^N$$
$$+ \qquad \longrightarrow \text{R} \begin{array}{l} \text{WALK} \\ \text{REACH} \\ \text{PUT IN PAN} \end{array} \longrightarrow \text{S}^R \text{ HOT DOG}$$
$$\text{S}^D \begin{array}{l} \text{HOT DOG} \\ \text{VISIBLE} \end{array}$$

VERBAL CASE

$$\text{DEP}^N \longrightarrow \text{Rv} \begin{array}{l} \text{"MAY I HAVE} \\ \text{A HOT DOG"} \end{array} \longrightarrow \text{S}^R \text{ HOT DOG}$$

in an impossible situation. Remember that you agreed that a hot dog is a discriminative stimulus for the Rv "hot dog," and now you want to say that the Rv "hot dog" is also strong in the absence of the discriminative stimulus of the hot dog. If both controlled the Rv "hot dog," a person would be in the position of saying "hot dog" at all times, whether the hot dog were there or not. Also, many discriminative stimuli are absent at all times, yet we only mand some absent items at some times. So, absence *as such* cannot be the controller of the Rv "hot dog" when no hot dog is there.

Sometimes when there are no giant pandas, nor Sherman tanks, nor square roots of two around us, either you or I may speak of them. The problems of talking about, or naming, absent stimuli are very serious. We agreed that the mere absence of the stimulus isn't sufficient to produce the Rv. Some other variable or variables must be exercising control. We will have to look at this problem in more detail later, but for now we can see that deprivation is the source of control in some cases, such as when the Rv is part of a mand.

Mands are most like nonverbal operants, which is why we started with them. (1) They are controlled by deprivation or aversive stimulation; motivation is important. (2) They have narrowly defined consequences; if the Rv specifies milk, milk is what is produced, not beer. Most nonverbal operants are this way too, in the sense that a narrowly delimited set of consequences (a food pellet, thirty seconds without electric shock, etc.) are correlated with responses of moderately delimited effects and topographies (key-pecks, bar-presses). (3) But unlike the nonverbal operants, mands are formally independent of the speaker's discriminative stimuli.

DIAGNOSING MANDS

Can we say which Rv's are mands and which are not? Technically, and strictly speaking, a mand is a verbal operant, and as such requires both a controlling variable and a Rv. So, no Rv in itself is a mand. But we can do better than just this. Some Rv's can be immediately ruled out as not being parts of mands. For example, "however," "3.1417," and "stock market crashes" are not mands. But there is no Rv whose occurrence uniquely and reliably indicates the occurrence of a mand. This is because all Rv's that occur in mands are also parts of verbal operants that are not mands. Just look at our previous examples of mands and figure out cases where the Rv's wouldn't be parts of mands. Here is a hint: If you read them aloud, the Rv's are not mands; they are parts of textuals (to be defined and explained later). But, for any Rv that is a part of more than one operant, an inference can be made from the context in which it occurs. We all do this, because we are all reinforcement mediators. Thus, if we hear the Rv "hot dog," we may ask, Is it a mand? It could be, and to judge, we examine the context in which it occurs. If said in the presence of a vendor at a baseball park, it probably is; if said just after the discriminative stimulus "What did you have to eat," it probably isn't part of a mand.

SUPPLEMENTARY STRENGTHENING
AND THE IMPURE MAND

Because a Rv, for example the Rv "hot dog," may be part of a mand on one occasion and not on another, diagnosis is difficult. Furthermore, it seems that the Rv "hot dog" may occur on one occasion for *two* reasons: (1) deprivation may be in effect, and (2) a discriminative stimulus, the hot dog itself, may be present. This is called SUPPLEMENTARY STRENGTHENING. IT OCCURS IF TWO OR MORE CONTROLLING VARIABLES IN TWO OR MORE OPERANTS THAT SHARE THE SAME Rv ARE PRESENT AT THE SAME TIME; THE EFFECT ON THE PROBABILITY OF THE Rv IS ADDITIVE. Therefore a Rv may occur for several reasons, one of which is deprivation, and the others of which are likely to be discriminative stimuli. Of course, the two or more controlling variables could be all deprivations, or they could be all discriminative stimuli.

TO THE EXTENT THAT SOME VARIABLE OTHER THAN DEPRIVATION OR AVERSIVE STIMULATION IS EXERTING CONTROL OVER THE Rv (CONTRIBUTING TO ITS PROBABILITY OF OCCURRENCE), THE MAND IS SAID TO BE IMPURE. We may look at some examples of mands of differing degrees of purity. I'll describe them; you point out the deprivations and the discriminative stimuli.

> *Pure mand*: A man who hasn't eaten for a while lying in bed alone says aloud, "Pepperoni pizza with extra cheese"; or a dehydrated hermit alone in the desert says, "Water."
>
> *Impure mand*: Some food deprivation, and a person who usually has food—"Do you, by chance, Christopher Robin, happen to have a jar of honey?" After a large meal—"That looks good; I'll have a large piece of the strawberry cream pie, please."
>
> *This next one isn't a mand at all:* SD "Pooh, what have you been eating?" + SD three empty quart jars; Rv (in a sticky voice) "Honey."

Nearly all mands controlled by aversive stimulation are impure because an unconditioned or a conditioned negative reinforcer is also likely to function as a discriminative stimulus. The elephant that stands on your foot is a visual discriminative stimulus as well as an unconditioned negative reinforcer. There is just that very large, public discriminative stimulus which cannot be gotten rid of. Pure mands are, no doubt, very rare. Usually something else shows up. That's OK; pure mands still exist occasionally. We defined the pure case and showed that it was possible. If we find other causal variables at work, so much the better. We are in good shape if behavior has several causes rather than none at all.

Something like the typical impure mand can be shown in the pigeon's behavior. We may keep him in the pecking apparatus all the time and feed him any time he pecks. The key-peck is, then, functionally equivalent to the human's Rv "Food, please." But notice, the key-peck must be performed in a special place. The key is the bird's reinforcement mediator, and to a certain extent governs the form and locus of his response. Real verbal behavior acts at a distance and is free of environmental control over its form.

WHY DO SPEAKERS MAND?

For all operant classes, such as mands, we will have to explain why the speaker and the hearer do what they do. We have to exhibit the two sets of reinforcing contingencies. The reinforcement contingencies for the speaker are obvious and familiar in their dynamics. Manding is distinctly *interested* behavior. The speaker gets something out of it. We know what he gets by seeing which Rv he emitted. The reinforcement per unit of physical work is amazingly large. The magic of words was even more impressive before the advent of modern machinery, but even so, the advantages are still there. Compare the Rv "Give me a loaf of bread, please" with all the responses required to grow the wheat, mill it, milk the cow, mix the dough, and bake it. We can get reinforcers via mands that would otherwise be unobtainable. We merely mand "bread," "toothpaste," "color TV," "Mercedes-Benz." Some of the specialization of our society is made possible, in part, by the ability to mand.

Probably, the more important question is, "why don't people mand more than they do?" Bossy people and tyrants mand a lot; so did God, according to the Old Testament. The answer forms our next section.

WHY DOES THE HEARER COMPLY?

There are limits to the hearer's probability of complying (dispensing reinforcers). Everyone cannot mand everything because then no one would do anything. The roles of mander and reinforcement mediator must reverse every once in a while. All the mands don't go into a few hands, because the complier must be reinforced for complying. As Skinner has put it, the mand is an imposition on the hearer. He spends more energy than the mander does; he often loses property. There is only one way to keep him doing all that—reinforce him for doing it.

Complying by the hearer increases the probability that the speaker will "pay him back" when each has the other's job to do. Not every speaker will do this every time. But, overall, complying increases this probability. However, the role reversal is likely to be delayed, and thus would be a very weak reinforcer. Therefore, the mander gives immediate reinforcement in the form of gratitude or promises or general acknowledgment of indebtedness. These, of course, are conditioned reinforcers which are correlated with other unconditioned reinforcers. The next illustration depicts this interchange again, and names some of the possible conditioned reinforcers. Obviously, one of the best conditioned reinforcers is money. We know that it can be traded in at any time that its recipient wants to mand. Our only supposition here is that "Thank you," smiles, pats, nods, kisses, and so forth, are functionally somewhat like money. If you think they have no similarity, I suggest that you consider whom you reinforce with "Thank you"—friends or total strangers? And I argue that one of the characteristics of friends is that you will be willing to reverse the roles with them. Thus a "Thank you" from a friend is more *valuable* than a "Thank you" from a stranger.

$$
\begin{array}{llll}
\text{MANDER:} & R_v \overset{\text{"MAY I HAVE}}{\text{A HOT DOG"}} \longrightarrow S^{r \cdot D} \overset{\text{HOT DOG}}{\text{IN HAND}} \longrightarrow R &
\begin{array}{l}\text{"THANK YOU"}\\\text{SMILE}\\\text{KISS}\\\text{"I'LL PAY YOU BACK"}\\\text{"I'LL GET THE NEXT}\\\quad\text{ONE"}\\\text{MONEY}\end{array}\\[2em]
\text{MEDIATOR:} & S^R \longrightarrow R^{\text{GIVE}} \longrightarrow S^r
\end{array}
$$

Another reason for the hearer's complying is that refusal may generate aversive stimulation. The next illustration depicts this paradigmatically and shows several examples of the sorts of aversive stimuli that may ensue when the hearer refuses to comply. Compliance is a form of avoidance behavior; its reinforcement consists in stopping the mand (terminating a conditioned negative reinforcer) and preventing the aversive consequences of noncompliance.

MANDER: Rv $^{"MAY\ I\ HAVE}_{A\ HOT\ DOG"}$ ⟶ $S^{r-\cdot D}$ ⟶ R $\begin{array}{l}\text{REPEAT LOUDER}\\\text{WHEEDLE}\\\text{HARP, SNIVEL}\\\text{WHINE, "AFTER ALL}\\\text{I'VE DONE FOR YOU"}\\\text{PHYSICAL ATTACK}\end{array}$

MEDIATOR: S^D ⟶ Rv$^{"NO"}$⟶ S^{r-}

In extreme cases the mand may have explicit collateral aversive stimulus properties, as shown in the next illustration. All mand situations are probably combinations of the elements shown in the next to last and next illustrations, that is, both positive and negative conditioned reinforcement are operative. I suspect that all mands are in some degree aversive to the hearer, although sometimes the subsequent reinforcement for complying may be positive as well as negative.

MANDER: Rv $^{"YOUR\ MONEY}_{OR\ YOUR\ LIFE"}$ ⟶ $S^{r\cdot D}$ $\xrightarrow{MONEY}$ R LEAVES

MEDIATOR: $S^{r-\cdot D}$ ⟶   R$\xrightarrow{GIVES}$ S^{r-} ENDS

ALSO

MANDER: Rv $\begin{array}{l}\text{"SPARE A QUARTER"}\\\text{"I AIN'T HAD ANYTHING TO EAT"}\\\text{"MY KIDS...."}\\\text{"MY WIFE...."}\end{array}$ ⟶ $S^{r\cdot D}$ ⟶ R $^{GOES}_{AWAY}$

MEDIATOR: $S^{r-\cdot D}_{DIRTY}$ + $S^{r-\cdot D}$ ⟶   R$\xrightarrow{GIVES}$ S^{r-}ENDS
$\phantom{MEDIATOR: S^{r-\cdot D}_{D}}$SMELLY

A fourth reason for complying is that mands sometimes consist of "advice." The hearer may be himself reinforced rather immediately and directly by his own behavior in complying. Skinner has said: "Advice is full of promises of reinforcers." These Rv's imply that the hearer will be reinforced for complying, as diagramed in the next illustration. When I *ask for* advice, I mand you to mand to me so that I am reinforced for complying

MANDER: Rv $\begin{array}{l}\text{"STOP"}\\\text{"TURN HERE"}\\\text{"JUMP"}\\\text{"GET ON THIS LINE"}\\\text{"REREAD THIS BOOK"}\end{array}$

MEDIATOR: S^D ⟶ R ⟶ S^R OR S^r

with your mand. Invitations follow the same paradigm, such as in the Rv "Come to dinner." A hearer who gets a lot of these discriminative stimuli may develop a disposition to comply with mands. Skinner has suggested that "a good mander slips one of these sorts of mands in from time to time." Such mands, along with advice, produce an individual who is generally likely to comply with all sorts of mands. He does this because of those occasional reinforcements that follow complying with the special advice and invitation mand forms.

Finally, the hearer has usually been, as Skinner has put it, "softened up." Mands, nowadays, seldom come in raw form; we request, and do not order. Bryant and Aiken have given many examples of this, and we list some here:

"Please give me a hot dog"
"Do give me a hot dog"
"Would you mind giving me a hot dog"
"Will you please give me a hot dog"
"Could you give me a hot dog, please"
"Would you like to give me a hot dog"
"Won't you give me a hot dog"
"Do you want to give me a hot dog"
"Would you care to give me a hot dog"
"Might I ask you to give me a hot dog"
"Let me beg of you to give me a hot dog"
"May I ask you to give me a hot dog"
"I should be glad if you would give me a hot dog"
"Please do me the favor of giving me a hot dog"
"May I trouble you to give me a hot dog"
"Let me request you to give me a hot dog"
"Give me a hot dog, if you please"
"I would like you to give me a hot dog"
"May I suggest that you give me a hot dog"
"Would it be too much to ask you to give me a hot dog"
"Would you be good enough to give me a hot dog"
"Please to give me a hot dog"
"Would you please give me a hot dog"
"Wouldn't you like to give me a hot dog"
"I would be happy if you would give me a hot dog"
"I should like you to give me a hot dog"

"Would you be kind enough to give me a hot dog"

"I would appreciate your giving me a hot dog"

"I should appreciate your giving me a hot dog"

"I would be grateful if you would give me a hot dog"

"I should be grateful if you would give me a hot dog"

"I would consider it a favor if you would give me a hot dog"

"I would be eternally grateful if you would give me a hot dog"

"I cannot tell you how much I would appreciate it if you would give
me a hot dog"

"I would be greatly relieved if you would give me a hot dog"

These seem to increase overall compliance as a kind of generalized disposition (tendency). They are also full of promise; they give the complier an opportunity to do some very reinforceable thing.

DEPRIVATION AND AVERSIVE STIMULATION AS SUPPLEMENTARY VARIABLES

We have already seen that pure mands are few and far between. Most mands are impure because any Rv may be evoked by more than one variable. So, an ordinarily weak deprivation, which exerts some weak control over a Rv, but which by itself wouldn't evoke the Rv, may produce the Rv if some stimulus that also controls the same Rv is concurrently present. Additionally, deprivation and aversive stimulation may help evoke a Rv in a non-mand situation. This is not a case of impure mands. Here we start out with deprivation or aversive stimulation without any control over the Rv in question. (Of course, if reinforcement then ensues, mands may be created and tend to recur.) Ambiguous stimuli, such as those presented in the various projective tests (e.g., the TAT or the Rorschach), produce Rv's, for example, "fried chicken." These Rv's are usually parts of tacts (soon to be discussed), not mands. Intensifying deprivation or aversive stimulation increases the probability of these Rv's. But, such Rv's aren't parts of mands because they do not specify their reinforcers and they are not the basis for conventional compliance by a reinforcing community. They are not under the control of deprivation or aversive stimulation here. They would not occur without the discriminative stimuli present. All that the deprivation or aversive stimulation does is "amplify" the controlling power of the discriminative stimuli, that is, increase momentarily and temporarily the strength of the arrow between the S^D and the Rv.

THE SELF AS MEDIATOR

Can the mander and the mediator be one and the same person? It seems that they can. As a result of having been conditioned to (1) mand, and (2) mediate, by someone else, we play both roles to others and to ourselves. Adults, as accomplished mander-compliers, seem to approach everything as if it were a verbal problem, and they then use the Rv:S^D's to cue nonverbal responses. The next illustration presents an example. Here both the mander (the speaker) and the mediator (the doer) are reinforced by the same event. But note that the mediator is always reinforced first and fastest. The mediating operants finally get stronger than the mands, which are then crowded out. This is because the Rv's of the mands are parasitic (dependent on the occurrence and reinforcement of the nonverbal behavior for their reinforcement). It is the mediating behavior that is doing all the work. The self as mediator is just the advice case again, with both roles going on in the same body.

$$Rv^{\text{"HEAD DOWN"}} : S^D \longrightarrow R_{\text{HEAD}}^{\text{LOWER}} : S^D \longrightarrow Rv^{\text{"ELBOW STRAIGHT"}} : S^D \longrightarrow R_{\text{ELBOW}}^{\text{STRAIGHTEN}} : S^D \longrightarrow$$

$$Rv^{\text{"EYE ON BALL"}} : S^D \longrightarrow R^{\text{LOOK}} : S^D \longrightarrow \quad . \quad . \quad . \quad S^r \; \substack{375 = \text{YARD} \\ \text{HOLE IN ONE}}$$

ANOMALOUS MANDS

We now come to a mixed collection of cases which seem to be mands because they "specify their reinforcers." Yet, because they appear in situations for which a past history of mediated reinforcement is not plausible or possible, it is doubtful that any mediator ever complied. The classes that follow may not have distinct boundaries; they may overlap to some extent. The names of the classes and their definitions are, of course, Skinner's inventions.

GENERALIZED MANDS TO NONREINFORCING AUDIENCES: THESE ARE MANDS ADDRESSED TO INANIMATE OR NONVERBAL (NONCOMPLYING) AUDIENCES, AUDIENCES THAT HAVE NEVER BEEN CONDITIONED TO COMPLY.

To baby: "Wave bye-bye."
To stray dog: "Go home."
In desert: "Water."
To onrushing car: "Stop."
To table: "Get out of the way."

But these Rv's have been reinforced in similar situations before. So, stimulus generalization could account for their occurrence. Remember that stimulus generalization is the tendency for a response to occur to stimuli that have not been involved in original conditioning. Stimulus generalization can be shown by the pigeon if we vary the color of the light on the key. If the bird was originally reinforced for pecking a yellow light, he will peck less if the light becomes orange or red or green, although he will have some tendency to peck at colors similar to the one involved in conditioning. We do not seem to have to arrange for this; it appears to be a built-in tendency. Stimulus generalization also occurs in humans and shows up in verbal behavior.

SUPERSTITIOUS MANDS ARE THOSE THAT HAVE BEEN ESTABLISHED THROUGH ACCIDENTAL OR ADVENTITIOUS REINFORCEMENT IN THE PAST. The verbal behavior of gamblers provides most of the examples: "Come seven" (to dice), "Go, boy, go" (to horse on TV), "Not there, not there" (to roulette ball).

WRITTEN MANDS ARE JUST WRITTEN RESPONSES WHICH WHEN READ ALOUD SEEM TO BE PARTS OF MANDLIKE OPERANTS. I will not try to explain them. First of all, written mands do not constitute vocal verbal behavior, our subject matter here. Second, their controlling variables may be different. Third, in the case of the written mand there usually appears to be no audience present. Hence, there does not appear to be any likelihood of reinforcement, and the probability of the response ought to be low. Skinner, however, knows how to solve these problems, so if you are interested in the extension of this sort of analysis to writing, you might read *Verbal Behavior.*

MAGICAL MANDS OCCUR WHEN THERE IS NO POSSIBILITY OF THE RESPONSE EVER HAVING YIELDED COMPLIANCE, EVEN THOUGH THE Rv SPECIFIES ITS REINFORCER AND WE PROVISIONALLY DIAGNOSE IT AS PART OF A MAND. Emotional behavior cannot be successfully manded. We say "Don't cry," but she continues to do so; we say "Weep for Adonais," but nobody does. The Satanist calls the devil, or the witch doctor exorcises demons, but no one comes or goes. Why? These aren't mands. Magical mands are a product of response induction. RESPONSE INDUCTION IS ANOTHER UN-CONDITIONED PROCESS THAT OCCURS IN BOTH PIGEONS AND PEOPLE. IT IS THE TENDENCY FOR RESPONSES THAT ARE SOMEWHAT DIFFERENT FROM THE ONE THAT WAS REINFORCED TO OCCUR. If the pigeon was reinforced for pecking the key with a force of 10 grams, there is a tendency for pecks of different forces to occur. Sometimes the peck will have a force of 12 grams, sometimes 8, sometimes 14, sometimes 9, and so forth. So, just as pecks may vary in their properties, Rv's may vary too.

Some odds and ends: Questions are usually mands, except for the rhetorical ones and the student's repeating the question while he is working on the answer. The answer to a question is usually a discriminative stimulus which allows the questioner, the mander, to act so as to be reinforced by deprivation dependent stimuli or the elimination of aversive stimulation, as in "Where is the men's room?" Cursing is also a form of manding under the control of aversive stimulation: "Go to the devil." Gay Wilson Allen said that in the William James family a favorite mand was, "May you always have lumps in your mashed potatoes."

4

tacts

DEFINITION AND PARADIGM

A TACT IS A VERBAL OPERANT WHOSE ANTECEDENT IS AN ENVIRONMENTAL EVENT OR STATE OF AFFAIRS (DISCRIMINATIVE STIMULUS) AND WHOSE REINFORCEMENT HAS BEEN CONTINGENT UPON A CONVENTIONAL CORRESPONDENCE BETWEEN THE DISCRIMINATIVE STIMULUS AND THE Rv, THAT IS, THE PRESENCE OF THE DISCRIMINATIVE STIMULUS AND A CHARACTERISTIC CONVENTIONAL Rv FORM (TOPOGRAPHY).

This definition says that there is a tendency for speech to change as objects and events in the speaker's environment change. Certain Rv's are conventional for certain states of the environment; if both are present, then the reinforcement mediator reinforces. Notice that here the reinforcement mediator has been conditioned to reinforce some verbal behavior *not* on the basis of the Rv alone, as he did for mands, nor on the basis of the discriminative stimulus, but simply because there is a *match* or *correspondence* according to the verbal community's conventions between the Rv and some aspect of the speaker's environment. If there is no such correspondence, the mediator doesn't reinforce. The product of the differential reinforcement contingency is a tact. Tacts are operants under discriminative control; they are said to be "objective." Their control is almost totally by discriminative stimuli; the behavior may be said to be "disinterested" or "unselfish." The next two illustrations display the tact and its reinforcement history paradigmatically. The first illustration emphasizes that the tact, like the mand, is

$$\underbrace{S^D \longrightarrow Rv}_{TACT}$$

also an operant, with three parts: (1) a relation between (2) an antecedent controlling variable, in this case only a discriminative stimulus, and (3) a Rv. The second illustration emphasizes the fact that the three parts of the

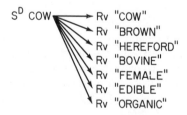

speaker's tact together constitute the discriminative stimulus for the reinforcement mediator. This discriminative stimulus for the mediator causes him to respond. And, this response by the mediator serves as, or directly produces, a reinforcer for the speaker which serves to thereby strengthen the controlling relation (arrow) between the discriminative stimulus and the Rv of the speaker's tact. The next illustration shows some examples of common tacts. The left side indicates the physical discriminative stimulus;

$$S^D \text{ BUILDING} \longrightarrow Rv \text{ "BUILDING"}$$
$$S^D \text{ GRASS} \longrightarrow Rv \text{ "GRASS"}$$

$$S^D \text{ COW} \nearrow Rv \text{ "COW"}$$
Rv "BROWN"
Rv "HEREFORD"
Rv "BOVINE"
Rv "FEMALE"
Rv "EDIBLE"
Rv "ORGANIC"

the right, the Rv. In the third example we see an important fact illustrated: One physical item (discriminative stimulus), the cow, serves as the antecedent controlling variable for seven Rv's, and hence, in this illustration is part of seven tacts.

In all cases of tacting, the probability that these Rv's will occur (be spoken), is higher in the presence of these things (discriminative stimuli) than in their absence. Naming, of course, is the most obvious sort of tacting.

This may now sound a little peculiar, but please notice that the form of the Rv in naming is not at all like the form of the discriminative stimulus. There was once a theory of language acquisition that said otherwise. That theory said that the sound of the Rv (the *word*) is like the sound of the discriminative stimulus (the thing itself). Such a theory might simplify our account if it were true, but it is not. To see this, consider "house" and "horse," which as Rv's sound similar but sound and look different as things. Consider also "house" and "maison," which as Rv's sound different but *refer to* (are controlled by) the same thing. Also, the thing (house), as a discriminative stimulus, may be sufficient to evoke (control) the Rv's "glass," "windows," "doors," "siding," "porch," and so forth, none of which Rv's sound like or look like the discriminative stimulus. Notice also that one antecedent controls many Rv's, as in the last example in the preceding illustration. The conventional match, as you can easily see, does not require the same word for both the discriminative stimulus and the Rv.

Our definition of tact is much more general than the traditional view of naming. Other, more interesting—and more troublesome—Rv's for traditional views of language, are parts of tacts. The next illustration shows

S^D A PERSON MEETS ME FOR FIRST TIME THAT DAY $\longrightarrow$ Rv "GOOD MORNING"

S^D PUNISHMENT $\longrightarrow$ Rv "DRAT"
$\longrightarrow$ Rv "BOTHER"

S^D PHONE BELL $\longrightarrow$ Rv "HELLO"

some examples of these nonnaming tacts. These contain speech that is dependent upon an occasion for its appropriateness (reinforcement); they also have inappropriate instances in which no reinforcement will be forthcoming. These tacts do not name, describe, refer, mean, "verbally point," or "suggest aboutness." So, although many tacts seem to be like what has traditionally been viewed as reference or denotation, tacting is not a paraphrase of these notions. Tacting generally does include the cases that have been treated by those notions. But it includes many things that the traditional concepts omit.

WE SHOULD DISTINGUISH BETWEEN ANNOUNCEMENTS, WHICH ARE SIMPLE SINGLE TACTS, AND ASSERTIONS, WHICH ARE COMPOUNDS OF SEVERAL TACTS AND SOME OTHER THINGS. For example, announcements: "red," "house," "dog," "Fred"; assertions: "The house is red," "Fred is a dog," "Fred is in the doghouse again." How the other things get there and how they are combined is a story for a later chapter.

REINFORCEMENT FOR TACTING

A reinforcing community consists of several people who tend to behave in the same way. They will engage in reinforcing behavior when some sounds occur in a certain environment. That is what we meant by "a conventional match between a discriminative stimulus and a Rv." That interaction is paradigmatically shown in the illustration on page 41. To the extent that someone reinforces, a tact is created or strengthened. Because any sound can be made in any environment, the precision of the match between the Rv and the discriminative stimulus is usually required to be fairly strict. But some deviance is tolerated in shaping up the behavior of less than fully conditioned speakers, as shown in the next two illustrations. The first

(1) S^D AUTOMOBILE ⟶ Rv "CAR" ⟶ S^r "RIGHT"

        S^D TRUCK ⟶ Rv "CAR"

        S^D BUS ⟶ Rv "CAR"

SPEAKER: S^D FIRE ENGINE ⟶ Rv "CAR" } $\overset{?}{\longrightarrow} S^r$

        S^D AMBULANCE ⟶ Rv "CAR"

        S^D MOTOR HOME ⟶ Rv "CAR"

MEDIATOR: $S^D \overset{?}{\longrightarrow} R$ "YES"
                                              "GOOD"
                                              "TRUE"
                                              "THAT'S RIGHT"
                                              "GOOD BOY"

(2) SPEAKER: S^D CAR ⟶ Rv "BAR"
                                "FAR"
                                "KA"
                                "CHA" $\overset{?}{\longrightarrow} S^r$

MEDIATOR: $S^D \overset{?}{\longrightarrow} R$

illustration shows that when the speaker is a child or a foreigner—a person "learning to talk"—any one of several discriminative stimuli will serve in a *conventional match* with the Rv "car." That is, the reinforcement mediator will reinforce when this speaker makes that one Rv in the presence of any of these discriminative stimuli. The second illustration indicates that some variation in the Rv's form may be allowed. That is, Rv's that do not meet the verbal community's criteria for conventional correspondence between the discriminative stimulus and the Rv may be followed by reinforcement if the speaker is discriminated by the reinforcement mediator as not being a fully conditioned speaker (a person who is just learning).

Especially in the case of children, the reinforcement community will accept less than exact correspondences as occasions for reinforcement. Furthermore, the Rv form will be allowed some variation, initially. The community acts in an opportunistic way; when an approximation to the desired Rv form occurs, or the Rv occurs in the presence of something like the discriminative stimulus, the reinforcement is delivered. Things are cleaned up later. Once you get the speaker going, it is easier to sharpen up either the Rv or the correspondence. That's the essence of "shaping."

These processes are not limited to the interactions of children and adults. "Learning to talk" is not exclusively child's work. Tacts are acquired throughout life. Educated people learn many tacts after they are sixteen, and students in medical schools and graduate schools spend most of their time in their twenties learning tacts. Nor is adult acquisition of tacting limited to the professional experts. The man from New York City has to learn some new tacts when he gets out West, as shown in the next illustration. Many of us in the over-the-hill generation learned to tact such things

as grommet, gantry, vapor trail, command module, transistor, rille, laser, and computer long after people had stopped teaching us to talk and we were over our development and into our senescence.

By definition the Rv in a tact is controlled, in both its form and its probability, by a discriminative stimulus. It is *objective*. Pure tacts do exist; other variables have been kept out. TO SAY THAT A TACT IS PURE MEANS THAT THE REINFORCING COMMUNITY HAS BEEN ABLE TO REINFORCE TACTING WITHOUT GIVING THE SPEAKER'S ANTECEDENT MOTIVATION (DEPRIVATION OR AVERSIVE STIMULATION) CONTROL. Wholly *disinterested* tacting does occur. A horse is tacted as such whether the speaker is hungry or thirsty or cold or wet or, as N. R. Hanson said, is "sitting there, fat, dumb, and happy."

Objective, disinterested tacting is created by avoiding the use of any reinforcers that depend on deprivation for their effectiveness (food, water, air, etc.). If one avoids such reinforcers, deprivation won't be present when the Rv is reinforced and thus won't gain some control over it. Also, one avoids any stimuli that have been exclusively established as means to some deprivation-dependent unconditioned reinforcer, that is, any simple conditioned reinforcers. The reason is that simple conditioned reinforcers depend on deprivation for their effectiveness, too, and they pose the same problems as do the unconditioned reinforcers. And, finally, one has to stay entirely away from negative reinforcers of any sort, because they have those conspicuous discriminative stimuli compounded with them.

What are left, and what are used, are the CONDITIONED GENERALIZED REINFORCERS. THESE ARE STIMULI THAT HAVE BEEN PAIRED WITH, OR ESTABLISHED AS MEANS TO, MANY OTHER REINFORCERS, BOTH CONDITIONED AND UNCONDITIONED. The generalized conditioned reinforcers neither reduce nor depend upon any particular deprivation condition for their effectiveness. Nor do they vary with deprivation or aversive stimulation. The next illustration shows some examples in the paradigm.

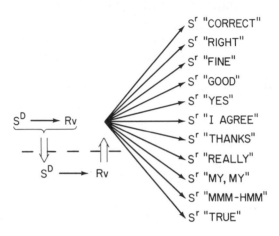

Another good generalized conditioned reinforcer is money. It seems to reinforce at any time, totally irrespective of deprivation, because it is a means to all other reinforcers, positive or negative, conditioned or unconditioned. We know why the verbal conditioned generalized reinforcers listed in the preceding illustration work. We suppose that they have been correlated with many other reinforcers, the way money has. Furthermore, some nonverbal generalized conditioned reinforcers may be used in the same way, for the same reasons, such as nods, smiles, pats on the head, upraised thumbs. And, finally, some punishment may be used for inexact correspondences, such as ridicule, contempt: "No, no; not a horse, a pig, Don't you know anything?"

Many experiments have shown that conditioned reinforcers may be used to increase the probability of selected Rv's. The strengthening of arbitrarily selected operants is the one area of experimental research in verbal behavior that is based on Skinner's analysis. Holz and Azrin review and summarize these studies in their chapter in the book edited by Honig, which is listed in the References. Here are brief descriptions of two classic studies which have shown the effectiveness of conditioned reinforcers on verbal behavior. Greenspoon found that if he asked college students to just talk (say words) and followed selected Rv's with the sound "mmm-hmm" made by him, the frequency of those Rv's increased in subsequent speech by the students. This occurred despite the fact that Greenspoon did nothing else when each student was speaking. Hildum and Brown found that if they made the Rv "good" over the telephone, they could bias people's responses to questions on attitudes toward general education courses at Harvard University. We should, however, be aware that some dubiety has been expressed with regard to certain studies that have demonstrated the reinforcing power of stimuli such as "mmm-hmm." Most of the reservations and controversies are about whether or not the speaker may have to be "aware" of the contingencies of the experiment in order that the stimulus increase the frequency of the selected Rv. There is little need for the Skinnerian to worry. The necessity for *awareness* does not disqualify stimuli such as "mmm-hmm" from being placed in the category of reinforcers. They do, after all, increase Rv frequency when they are dispensed following the selected Rv's. Furthermore, *awareness* is only required if the response class is badly chosen.

The earliest experiment I know of that used operant conditioning principles on verbal behavior was reported in the unpublished Ph.D. thesis of Dr. Kay W. Estes. Rather than rely upon any verbal reinforcers, Dr. Estes constructed some specifically for her experiment. They consisted of the movement of the single hand of a specially made cuckoo clock. When the hand moved, a bell rang, and each time the hand moved to the twelve o'clock position a door on the clock opened and a small toy animal made of colored pipe cleaners was pushed out. Previous work showed that five-year-old children, who were the subjects of Dr. Estes's experiments, found the toys reinforcing. The children were not reinforced by the movements of the clock hand before they were paired with toy presentations. Thus, if clock-hand movements would increase the rate of emission of selected Rv's, it would be safe to conclude that they did so on the basis of being made reinforcers by being paired with or serving as a means to the toys.

To generate some verbal behavior upon which the reinforcers could be tested, Dr. Estes had to get the children to talk. She did this by showing each child a scrapbook in which were pasted pictures. Two or more people were shown in twenty-one of the pictures; two or more animals in six pictures; people telephoning or talking in nine pictures; people and animals in four pictures; and colored inkblots only in eight pictures. Each child was asked, "What is the man (the dog, the lady, the boy, etc., as appropriate) saying?" If in his response to Dr. Estes's question, the child included the Rv "please," the clock hand was advanced. The children, of course, were not told that anything that they did would advance the clock hand, although they were informed that they would be allowed to take the toys whenever the clock gave them one.

Dr. Estes found that the frequencies of Rv's of all sorts were increased by her experimental procedure. When she analyzed the children's responses, she found significant increases in the frequencies of Rv's that seemed to be parts of mands and those that seemed to be parts of tacts, as well as a great increase in the number of occurrences of the Rv "please." When the analysis was adjusted for the increase in the total number of Rv's produced by the reinforcement procedure, significant increases in the proportion of Rv's seeming to belong to mands and the proportion of Rv's of the form "please" occurred. Of the nine children in this part of this experiment, two were able to tell Dr. Estes what "made the clock work." The seven other children showed no ability to describe the contingencies of the experiment and denied knowing how to "make the clock work."

In a second similar experiment with ten other children, the Rv "want" was reinforced in the same way. Again, the frequency of Rv's of the form "want" increased markedly, as did the number of all Rv's and the number of Rv's that appeared to be parts of mands. I think that on the basis of experiments like these, we can be unperturbed about our use of the concept of conditioned reinforcement in our explanations of verbal behavior.

COMPARISON OF TACT AND MAND

With what we have thus far, we are in a position to compare the tact and the mand. The key to it all, really, is the difference in the reinforcement histories involved. The next illustration shows the differences between the two paradigms and the two reinforcement histories in two ways—first, by putting the two paradigms side by side, and, second, by comparing the two sorts of operants with respect to their component parts as listed in tabular form.

Reinforcement is contingent upon the Rv of the mand alone, as far as the reinforcing community is concerned. The Rv tells the mediator about the speaker's deprivation or aversive stimulation; the mediator doesn't have to know about them independently of the Rv. The reinforcers involved are specific to the Rv; they are not interchangeable. This sort of speech may be called self-interested or selfish.

Reinforcement for tacting, however, is contingent upon the correspondence between the discriminative stimulus and the Rv. The reinforcement community pays close attention to this. The reinforcers involved in creating tacting make up a short list but are interchangeable. Tacting is disinterested or objective. It tells us nothing about the speaker's deprivation unless he is specifically tacting it, as in "I haven't had anything to eat since last night" or "I just ate."

Some special cases appear to be *interested* tacts, but these usually are mands that are disguised as tacts so as to "soften up" the reinforcement mediator. Here are some examples. I am stimulated by an unconditioned

MAND:

$$DEP^N \text{ OR } S^{R-} \longrightarrow Rv \longrightarrow \begin{array}{c} S^r \text{ OR } S^{r-} \\ \text{OR} \quad \text{OR} \\ S^R \text{ OR } S^{R-} \end{array} \text{ TERMINATED}$$

$$S^D \longrightarrow R$$

TACT:

$$S^D \longrightarrow Rv \longrightarrow S^r$$

$$S^D \longrightarrow R$$

MAND	TACT
$Rv \longrightarrow S^r \text{ OR } S^R$ $\underbrace{S^{r-} \text{ OR } S^{R-}}\text{TERMINATE}$ SPECIFIC TO Rv	$S^D \longrightarrow Rv \longrightarrow S^r$ GENERALIZED INTERCHANGEABLE
IF Rv "HOT DOG, PLEASE", S^R IS HOT DOG, NOT BOLOGNA, HAMBURGER, LOLLIPOP, ICE CREAM, PIZZA, OR ROLLS ROYCE.	IF $S^D \xrightarrow{CAR} Rv$ "CAR" S^r "THANKS", S^r "RIGHT", S^r "GOOD", S^r "FINE", WORK, AND ALSO $S^D \xrightarrow{CAR} Rv$ "CAR" $\longrightarrow S^r$ "RIGHT" $S^D \xrightarrow{CAT} Rv$ "CAT" $\longrightarrow S^r$ "RIGHT" $S^D \xrightarrow{COP} Rv$ "COP" $\longrightarrow S^r$ "RIGHT" WORK

	MAND	TACT
CONTROLLING VARIABLE	DEPRIVATION AVERSIVE STIMULATION NO S^D's	S^D's NOT DEPRIVATION OR AVERSIVE STIMULATION
REINFORCER	SPECIFIED BY Rv S^R, S^{R-}, S^r, S^{r-} ONLY ONE PER MAND	INDEPENDENT OF Rv GENERALIZED Sr ONLY ANY S^r FOR ANY TACT ONE S^r FOR MANY TACTS
CORRESPONDENCE OF S^D AND Rv	NONE	EXACT
MOTIVATION OF SPEAKER	INTERESTED (MOTIVATED)	DISINTERESTED (UNMOTIVATED)
REQUIREMENT OF MEDIATOR	GIVE S^R SPECIFIED DON'T INQUIRE AS TO ANTECEDENT CONTROL	MAKE SURE Rv MATCHES S^D, WHICH GENERALIZED Sr DOESN'T MATTER MUST KNOW SPEAKER'S CONTROLLING VARIABLE

negative reinforcer and emit the Rv "The door's open." This is a mand. If you replied, "Oh yes, so it is; thanks for telling me," I might change the form of my mand, for example, "Close the door."

Motivation for tacting has been postulated by other accounts as if it were logically impossible for behavior to occur without some underlying drive or motivating state. It has been said that we have a need for self-expression, and that tacting reduces that need. If this theory were true, saying anything would satisfy the need, and it would be easy to learn and do. But lies and nonsense aren't common Rv's of people who are exposed to discriminative stimuli, politicians excepted. Also, because Rv's do covary with their environmental circumstances, they are not self-expressions; they express the environment. And, to the extent that tacting is a result of the activities of reinforcement mediators, it is an expression of conventions, not the speaker's self-expression.

WHY DO MEDIATORS PLAY THEIR ROLE?

At first blush, it is hard to see why mediators do what they do in reinforcing tacting. Anyone who plays the role of reinforcement mediator for tacting doesn't know any more after the speaker has spoken than he did on the basis of the discriminative stimulus alone. Yet he reinforces on the basis of the exact correspondence between the speaker's Rv and the discriminative stimulus. Doing all this seems to be a waste of his time and energy. However, if the members of the reinforcing community do their job properly, in most (ideal) cases, the tacter

1. Tacts exactly on the Rv side, i.e., the Rv has a specific form;
2. Will be completely under the control of discriminative stimuli and discriminative stimuli alone; he will speak if they are present, and be silent if they are absent;
3. Behaves disinterestedly from the standpoint of his own deprivations and aversive stimulations; and
4. Does all of the preceding whether the reinforcement mediator has access to the discriminative stimulus or not.

Therefore, by preparing exact tacters the mediator can vastly extend the functional range of his own senses. The tacter can often see, hear, or smell things that the mediator cannot. His tacts are not those stimuli, but his verbal behavior is a very direct, exact, known function of them. The next illustration shows the reinforcement accruing to the mediator in a para-

$$\text{SPEAKER} \quad S^D \longrightarrow Rv \longrightarrow S^r$$

$$- \ - \ - \ - \ -\Downarrow- \ -\Uparrow- \ - \ - \ -$$

$$\text{MEDIATOR} \qquad S^D \longrightarrow Rv \overset{\text{"THANKS"}}{}$$

$$\longrightarrow R \underset{\text{BEHAVIOR}}{\overset{\text{OTHER}}{}} \longrightarrow S^R$$

digmatic form. Here are some examples of Rv's from tacts; you should be able to figure out the nature of the discriminative stimulus for the tacting, the mediator's response, and his reinforcement:

"Lunch is ready."

"The suit you ordered is here."

"There's water in the cellar."

"The garbage man is here."

"I can let you have two hundred shares for a thousand dollars."

In short, as Skinner has said, "the mand is an imposition on the hearer; the tact is a favor to him." Anyway, that is usually the case. Different speakers keep us on different schedules. Babies are boring. They never tell us anything that we don't already know, but reinforcing their tacting is a good investment. Experts can see or hear discriminative stimuli that we cannot. They tact them for us. There are special subcommunities of other experts which reinforce the experts' tacting; that is how the tacting was generated. The other experts taught them how. Accurate tacting of real things that cannot be seen is part of science. The physicist does it when he tacts atoms and electrons. This kind of tacting is harder to acquire, and the distances between responses and reinforcements are longer. This does not mean that no discriminative stimuli control the physicist's behavior, but the relationships between the discriminative stimuli that control his tacts and his responses that "refer to" unobservables are very complicated. We need to know about textuals, intraverbals, and autoclitics before we can complete that story.

DISCRIMINATIVE STIMULI AS
SUPPLEMENTARY VARIABLES

Tacts show up in verbal behavior that is principally governed by something else. Examples of these are extremely common, and sportswriters and announcers specialize in producing things where one tact seems to intrude into another:

> "The Bengals clawed . . . "
> "The Pirates stole . . . "
> "The Cowboys rode over . . . "
> "The Broncos stampeded . . . "
> "The Indians scalped . . . "

Here are two not very funny ones that I manufactured:

> "His report hammered at the contrast between the strikers' and the managers' behavior."
> "His pitching made me want to throw up."

In utterances like these the speech is controlled by something else; it is not about vomiting or hitting things. Other Rv's might have occurred, such as "concentrated on," "emphasized," "pointed," "quit," "give up," "be sick," "go home." With all of these available, there is a problem of the resolution of the competition of the various possible responses with one another. What determines which Rv appears? A supplementary variable may help to solve this question, but more about that later.

DISTORTED TACTS: INEXACT CORRESPONDENCE

In the ideal tact, the mediator reinforces the speaker on the basis of the conventionality and exactness of the match between the latter's Rv and the discriminative stimulus. The mediator is indifferent to the specific discriminative stimuli and responses involved—what he cares about is whether they match according to the conventions of their reinforcing community. If this is all that happens, then all discriminative stimuli will be tacted with equal and great exactness and precision. However, the mediator does not always play his role properly. His principal temptation, and consequent defect, is to reinforce on the basis of the Rv alone, irrespective of its correspondence to the discriminative stimulus. The result is inexactness, unconventionality, and some distortion of the speaker's tacts. The purity of the tact is diluted, and it becomes a tact plus something else. There are several possibilities that produce some familiar products. Examples follow, grouped by the properties of the distorted tact's Rv.

Some Rv's are aversive and are not followed by reinforcement of the speaker. If the Rv is aversive to the mediator, he isn't likely to reinforce, no matter how good the correspondence between the Rv and the discriminative stimulus. The next illustration shows a paradigm for this. Sometimes the extinction of the tacter is permanent. In 2 *Samuel* 4:9-10, we are told that

David answered Rechab and Baanah: "As the Lord lives, who has redeemed my life out of every adversity, when one told me, 'Behold, Saul is dead,' and thought he was bringing me good news, I seized him and slew him at Ziklag, which was the reward I gave him for his news."—Not a nice boy, that David.

Other kinds of aversive Rv's are those that tact sex or excretory behavior, and many tactless tacts: "You are too fat," "You have dandruff," "I heard that your wife left you." These may be perfectly true and exact, but they remain weak. Euphemism and understatement may then occur and be reinforced: "It appears that you have a weight problem," "There seems to be some dust on your coat," "Perhaps you ought to know that there are rumors that things are not going well at home."

Palmer has tabulated many interesting euphemisms for cheap or unusual foods; here are some examples. The common Rv is on the left and the euphemistic Rv is on the right:

Fried fish	Bombay duck
Bag pudding	Leicestershire plover
Bread crust and garlic	Capon
Cow heel	Cobbler's lobster
Sheep's head stewed with onions	German duck
Red herrings	Norfolk capons
Red herrings	Gourock hams
Liver and potatoes	Poor man's goose
Shrimp	Gravesend sweetmeats
Potatoes	Irish apricots
Codfish	Cape Cod turkey
Sturgeon	Albany beef

Some Rv's are more useful, important, or interesting to the mediator than others are. This means that the probability, or magnitude, of the reinforcement, which results from the mediator's own behavior, for which the speaker's Rv is a discriminative stimulus, is greater. Such Rv's get preferential reinforcement from the mediator. If, in addition, the mediator has no access to the controlling variables for the speaker's behavior, inexactness is likely. *Exaggeration* may ensue: "an eighteen-inch mushroom," "a billionaire," "an absolutely perfect figure." Speech that produces special effects such as laugh getting or tear jerking occurs when the same discriminative stimulus may be tacted in several ways. But distortion is usually introduced by the special contingency these have with respect to the mediator's elicited, respondent, behaviors. They begin to specify their consequences, and become mandlike, even though they are still tacts. The ultimate case of distortion occurs when there is no discriminative stimulus for the Rv, according to the community's conventions, that is, *lying*. The man who cries wolf, or denies committing an action that he did perform, is manding. He mands generalized reinforcers in the first case (attention) and termination of aversive stimulation in the second.

Criteria of conventionality and exactness may differ in different reinforcing communities. Different mediators may reinforce different Rv's to the same set of discriminative stimuli. These differing communities, or audiences, have different conventions. A person who is a member of one audience may discriminate tacts that are exact, according to the conventions of the other, as distortions. Psychologists, for example, may be members of both the literary and the scientific audience, whereas English professors are likely to be members of the literary audience only. So, when the discriminative stimulus is a person, he can be tacted to the psychologists (scientific audience) in terms of MMPI, WAIS, CPI, Rorschach, and TAT scores, for example. Or he might be tacted with the Rv "He's a regular Scrooge." The literary audience says that the first set of tacts is lifeless jargon; it complains because tacts like these analyze to death, are far too complete, "leave nothing for the hearer to do." The scientific audience says that the "Scrooge" tact is untestable, inexact, and incomplete. The point is that the existence of distortion often depends upon the accepted conventionality of one's own verbal community, and there are many verbal communities within the larger one.

5

extended tacts

We have a parallel here with the mand. Namely, we find instances of tacts without, strictly speaking, a past history of reinforcement for emitting that Rv in the presence of that discriminative stimulus. When we encounter a new discriminative stimulus we are not always speechless—what we do is emit an old Rv, or part of an old Rv. We will discuss, in this chapter, cases of old responses to new or novel stimuli. My goal is, of course, to show you that such occurrences are still comprehensible within the restrictions we have placed upon our explanatory system.

TWO MECHANISMS

We can easily see that the verbal problem that we have been discussing in a preliminary way, just now, is a subclass of *stimulus generalization*. Let me repeat our definition of this: STIMULUS GENERALIZATION IS THE TENDENCY FOR STIMULI OTHER THAN THE ONE INVOLVED IN THE PAST HISTORY OF CONDITIONING TO EVOKE THE RESPONSE. WHEN THIS HAPPENS IN THE TACT CASE, WE SPEAK OF EXTENDED TACTS. We will consider two ways in which stimulus generalization occurs.

Simple stimulus generalization should be looked at first, in part because you already know about it. The next illustration gives a paradigm for simple stimulus generalization with the pigeon as the subject. If the pi-

PIGEON S^D YELLOW-GREEN ⟶ R PECK

TACT S^D BLUE ⟶ Rv "BLUE"

S^D NEXT YEAR'S CARS ⟶ Rv "CAR"

S^D THE SIDE VIEW OF FRED ⟶ Rv "FRED"

S^D FRED'S BROTHER SAM ⟶ Rv "FRED"

geon is conditioned to peck at a yellowish-green spot of light on the key, he continues to peck, but at lower rates as the light gets bluer (green, blue-green, blue, violet) or as it gets redder (yellow, yellow-orange, orange, red). This sort of effect may be observed, in general, for any stimuli on the same physical continuum, such as loudness, pitch, hue, or brightness. The same process also appears when the response is a Rv instead of a key-peck. The lower part of the preceding illustration shows this also. We will say "blue" to a band of colors, some of which we have never experienced before. Similarly, in the days of the annual model changes, next year's cars didn't leave us speechless, and a view of good old Fred from a new angle doesn't leave us with nothing to say.

STIMULI ALSO CLUSTER, AND TWO OR MORE COMPLEX STIMULI OR, MORE PROPERLY, CLUSTERS OF STIMULI, OFTEN HAVE COMMON ELE-MENTS. The next illustration shows the processes that go on here in para-

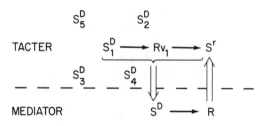

BUT AT THE SAME TIME

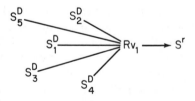

digmatic form. The reinforcement mediator discriminates the correspond-ence between discriminative stimulus 1 and Rv_1 and reinforces accordingly.

But, at the same time the total situation has other discriminative stimuli in it, and some of these may gain control over Rv_1. If some of the other discriminative stimuli (numbers two through five) have a fairly high frequency of accompanying discriminative stimulus 1, they may get a lot of control over Rv_1 because it gets reinforced in their presence too, and the situation depicted at the bottom of the illustration may result. The next illustration gives an example of extended tacts based on *whole-part clusters*. This is

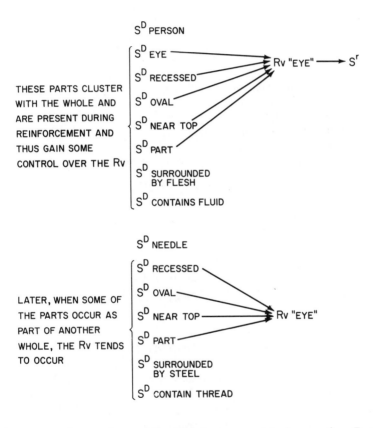

metaphor, a "figure of speech" which is supposed to be creative. But you see, the speaker does not create, instead stimuli control—by generalization. Furthermore, he is acting just like a pigeon. Many metaphors involve body parts, for example. If the discriminative stimulus is a projection from the body, the Rv "arm" gets reinforced, whether it is the arm of a man or the arm of a cross.

Simile is dynamically much the same as metaphor. We may say that a man is gentle as a lamb or that he is dumb as an ox. The next illustration shows the dynamics of the simile "gentle as a lamb." Simile and metaphor

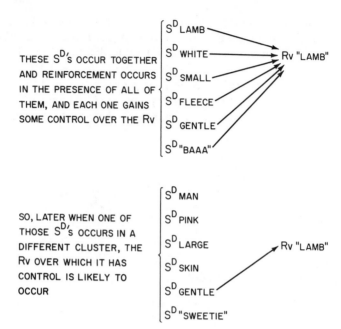

THESE S^{D}'s OCCUR TOGETHER AND REINFORCEMENT OCCURS IN THE PRESENCE OF ALL OF THEM, AND EACH ONE GAINS SOME CONTROL OVER THE Rv

S^{D} LAMB
S^{D} WHITE
S^{D} SMALL
S^{D} FLEECE
S^{D} GENTLE
S^{D} "BAAA"

Rv "LAMB"

SO, LATER WHEN ONE OF THOSE S^{D}'s OCCURS IN A DIFFERENT CLUSTER, THE Rv OVER WHICH IT HAS CONTROL IS LIKELY TO OCCUR

S^{D} MAN
S^{D} PINK
S^{D} LARGE
S^{D} SKIN
S^{D} GENTLE
S^{D} "SWEETIE"

Rv "LAMB"

are quite similar, but as the next illustration shows, in simile the common element is tacted twice.

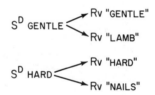

S^{D} GENTLE
Rv "GENTLE"
Rv "LAMB"

S^{D} HARD
Rv "HARD"
Rv "NAILS"

When the name of a part is evoked by the whole ensemble, we have a case of what is termed *synecdoche*. The next illustration shows this for a common folk expression, "I just hired two new hands." The processes illustrated here are a plausible reconstruction of what the original reinforcement history probably was. We do not learn these tacts in this way. For us the following Rv's are learned as echoics or textuals, but each was synecdoche for someone first:

"This part of the symphony is played by the strings."
"A herd of eighteen hundred head."
"His building has seven floors."
"A two-hundred-voice choir."

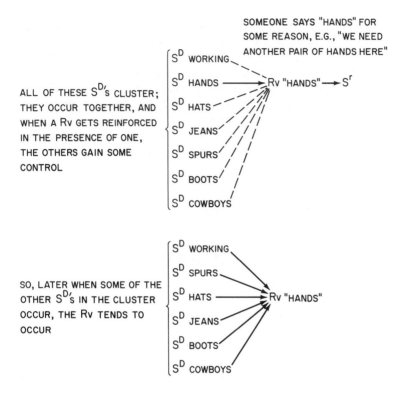

Metonymy is really just a special case of common elements clustering. It occurs when stimuli have *common accompaniments*. We can look at another of Skinner's examples. The president and the White House are common accompaniments; seeing one often leads us to speak of (tact) the other for very good reasons. We therefore have an exceptionally strong instance of metonymy in "The White House says . . . " Interestingly, it works only one way. When the presidential residence was being repaired during the Truman administration, no one said that they were "repainting the president," even though the Republicans claimed that the newspapers had "whitewashed" him during the freezer and mink coat scandals. There are plenty of other examples where metonymical extension is institutionalized: "The Chancellor's office says . . . ," "Wall Street is waiting for . . . ," "The Pentagon reports . . . ," "Seventh Avenue is looking for . . . "

Metonymy is not merely a literary curiosity and source of jokes. In large part it enables us to dispose of what is said to be a very difficult problem in verbal behavior. It allows us to explain tacting (speaking of) a missing discriminative stimulus. One explanation for the tacting of absent objects is that the dynamics of the metonymical situation are operating. The next illustration gives a paradigmatic example. When we were about to sit

down, my wife said (Rv), "There is no water on the table." Why did she say
(Rv) "water"? It is not part of a tact to the discriminative stimulus water,
nor is it a tact to the discriminative stimulus of no water, nor was it a mand
(she went to get the water). Remember, it won't do to say that absence of
water is also a state of the environment, so it served as a discriminative
stimulus for the Rv "no water." It is, indeed, a state of the environment,
but many, many other "absences" were there too, and she didn't tact them,
for example, no spiders, no trucks, no change, no George Washington
Bridge. The illustration shows how "water" gets said in this situation. It is

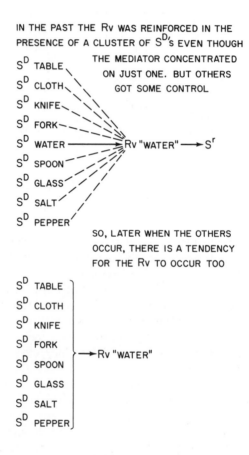

still the Rv of a tact, but it is evoked by water's common accompaniments.
The Rv's "there is" and "no" are still to be accounted for, because they are
under different sources of control and parts of different operants (autoclitics).

    Etymology is often a history of how a Rv of a tact got passed along
from discriminative stimulus to discriminative stimulus by the processes of

generalization which we have examined. The next illustration displays another of Skinner's examples. All these processes combine in new situations,

ORIGINALLY,

$$S^D \text{ KNIGHT} \longrightarrow Rv \text{ "SPUR"}$$

BUT ALSO S^D KNIGHT
$ S^D$ KICK HORSE $\longrightarrow Rv$ "SPUR"

SO, $\quad S^D$ KICK HORSE $\longrightarrow Rv$ "SPUR"

THEN, $\quad S^D$ KICK THING $\longrightarrow Rv$ "SPUR"

AND LATER

$$\begin{cases} S^D \text{ MOTIVATE} \longrightarrow Rv \text{ "SPUR"} \\ S^D \text{ EFFECT} \longrightarrow Rv \text{ "SPURT"} \\ S^D \text{ KICK AWAY} \longrightarrow Rv \text{ "SPURN"} \\ S^D \text{ SPUR-SHAPED THING} \longrightarrow Rv \text{ "SPUR OF RAILROAD"} \\ \phantom{S^D \text{ SPUR-SHAPED THING} \longrightarrow Rv} \text{ "SPUR OF BONE"} \\ \phantom{S^D \text{ SPUR-SHAPED THING} \longrightarrow Rv} \text{ "SPUR OF FLOWER"} \\ \phantom{S^D \text{ SPUR-SHAPED THING} \longrightarrow Rv} \text{ "SPAR OF BOAT"} \end{cases}$$

so the tacter is not speechless. But he is not creative either. Nor is his verbal behavior random. Whichever stimuli are available contribute strength to tacts or parts of them so that parts of old tacts occur.

DISCRIMINATION AND GENERALIZATION IN TACTING

If there were no processes opposing or limiting it, generalization (extension) could perhaps go on forever. Here is an example of what could happen. The Rv "nose" starts under the control of the discriminative stimulus nose of the man and then gets transferred by generalization to the following discriminative stimuli: nose of an airplane (metaphor)—all of the airplane (synecdoche)—all enclosures (generalization)—car—all moving things (more generalization)—everything. So, it would be possible to wind up with a one-word tact vocabulary, that is, "nose." We do have something like that with the Rv "thing." Although, in the case of the Rv "thing," the discriminative stimuli that control it also control other Rv's which at the same time allow for much more specific tacting. In the hypothetical nose example, "nose" is assumed to be the only Rv evoked by the stimuli. That sort of extended generalization would, however, make tacting useless to the hearer. Such tacting would not be a basis for effective (reinforced) behavior on the hearer's part. Imagine the plight of the poor hearer who gets the same Rv from the speaker irrespective of whether the discriminative stimulus is dinner on the table or a fire in the liquor cabinet.

Therefore the mediator must do something about this possibility. He heads it off. If tacting becomes too extended (generalized), the hearer does not reinforce the speaker. THIS PROCESS IS CALLED DISCRIMINATION. IT CONSISTS SOLELY OF THE NONREINFORCEMENT OF GENERALIZED RESPONSES. It is a way of whittling down the amount of generalization to a tolerable level. As Skinner put it, it will be useful for us to think of two opposing processes: (1) the speaker's tendency to generalize and extend his tacts and wind up with a one-word tact vocabulary; and (2) the hearer's tendency to reinforce only highly discriminated responses, and wind up with a speaker who utters proper names for things, and hence has a many word vocabulary. How the resolution of the opposing tendencies of these two processes is worked out is explained in detail in what follows. It, at one and the same time, satisfies the interests of both parties: The speaker gets to generalize, and the hearer receives highly discriminated tacts.

DEGREES OF DISCRIMINATION
IN TACTING

Two important subdivisions are considered here. The first, and most familiar, is *proper names.* PROPER NAMES ARE THE RV'S IN TACTS FOR A SMALL NUMBER OF SPECIAL, EASILY DISCRIMINATED, COMMONLY TACTED, ONE-OF-A-KIND DISCRIMINATIVE STIMULI. So very little generalization is allowed that if I give you the Rv, you can unfailingly locate the discriminative stimulus for it—for example, Howard Hughes, Ronald Reagan, San Francisco, Michelangelo's *David*, the Mona Lisa. These Rv's are in no way descriptive. Hence there is nothing that generalizes from a similar person, city, or object which would help the speaker in tacting. Tacts of this sort don't work if the hearer is *unfamiliar* with the discriminative stimulus—they don't work if he cannot locate the stimulus without help. That is the major part of the problem with proper-name tacts. Each one must always have its own complete reinforcement history, or the speaker won't speak it, or the hearer won't be able to respond to the speaker's Rv.

Although in some ways proper-name tacts are ideal for the hearer, proper naming in all tacts would have several serious defects. (1) Such a repertoire would take too much time and energy to acquire. (2) We would be speechless in new situations; the hearer would get only silence from us. (3) It requires the hearer to be familiar with the discriminative stimulus already; for example, he would have to know that the basement is flooded to respond to the proper name for that state of affairs. (4) Innocent generalization could lead to serious misunderstanding if proper naming were the only accepted mode of tacting. Someone who looks very much like the president, if improperly tacted at the wrong time or place, could start a nuclear war. "Sort of red" seems satisfactory as a tact to us, but "sort of Fred" does not. (5) Some discriminative stimuli are nearly indistinguishable; mass-produced objects probably wouldn't permit discriminations. Not only would every car have to have its own name (it does; the serial number or registration number), but so would all the frying pans, glasses, knives, forks, tables, chairs, pencils, and pens. We as tacters and hearers would just be overloaded.

How do we get around this? WE CAN GET ALL THE PRECISION OF PROPER-NAME TACTING BY A PROCESS OF REPEATED TACTING OF THE CON-TROLLING STIMULI. WE TACT THE DISCRIMINATIVE STIMULI IN TERMS OF THEIR OBJECT CLASS NAMES, THAT IS, THE NAMES OF THE CLASSES TO WHICH THE DISCRIMINATIVE STIMULUS BELONGS. WE ALSO LEARN TO TACT PROPERTIES OF OBJECTS, AND GENERALIZATION IS ALLOWED HERE, AS WELL AS WITH CLASS NAMES. So when we tact class names—e.g., book, ball, pen, tree, house—generalization is permitted; reinforcement still follows. Thus the same Rv "tree" can be made in the presence of familiar trees, unfamiliar trees, trees without leaves, trees with needles. The Rv "ball" will be reinforced in the presence of a red ball or a green one, a little one or a big one, a hard one or a soft one, and so on. The same sort of events occur with class names for groups. The Rv "forest" is reinforced for deciduous forests, for bamboo forests, for tropical forests, for evergreen forests, and for burned-over forests. As a result of this slack in the reinforcement contingencies, the speaker can tact a new or unfamiliar object on the basis of the similarity of the new discriminative stimulus to previous ones.

VERY SIMILAR PROCESSES GO ON IN THE TACTING OF THE ABSTRAC-TIONS (RESPONDING TO SINGLE ISOLATED PROPERTIES OF OBJECTS). For example, yellow, to the right of, loud, squeaky, are dimension class names. Generalization occurs here too, and on the same sort of bases: common elements or common physical dimensions. Thus generalization can occur to new values of the underlying physical dimension or to new combinations that include some of the elements previously present. For example, the speaker's Rv "loud" is reinforced when emitted in the presence of singing, gunshots, breaking china, subway trains, music, and so forth, whenever the discriminative stimulus has a relatively large sound pressure level. Reinforcement mediators allow plenty of variation. The Rv "yellow" is reinforced when emitted in the presence of yellow dresses, eggs, paper, or when it is orangy-yellow, yellow-yellow, greenish-yellow, bright yellow, or dim yellow, and so on. Therefore, generalization occurs here too.

Both the speaker and the reinforcement community can take advantage of all this generalization. The speaker can tact what is a new (to him) member of a previously experienced class. He may have been reinforced for tacting pigs (objects) and purples (properties), but never purple pigs previously. But, because generalization operates and hasn't been unduly constrained by discrimination training, he can now tact a new, strange purple pig.

Hearers can receive the functional equivalents of proper names through the speaker's complete or prolonged tacting of object class names or property names. If the speaker names enough subclasses or properties, he achieves a specificity equivalent to that of proper naming. Of course, he doesn't have to go all the way to that extreme. He can stop at some intermediate level that is a sufficient discriminative stimulus for the hearer's purposes, one that will allow the hearer to respond and be reinforced. Here is an example of such prolonged tacting. Remember, the discriminative stimulus remains the same for all of these Rv's: "shirt," "Fred's shirt," "Fred's new shirt," "Fred's new white shirt," "Fred's new white dress shirt," "Fred's new white dress shirt with the monogram," "Fred's new white dress shirt with the monogram which he is wearing now." That last utterance is (practically or functionally) a proper name. This process satisfies the speaker's interest (he can generalize) and the hearer's (he has to wait, but he gets the specificity of a proper name). This is a powerful process. It generates precise speech for all occasions, whether they be new or old.

We may notice that special problems of ambiguous tacting, which are like generalization, are generated in languages that have many *synonyms* or *homonyms*. The next illustration paradigmatically depicts these two effects.

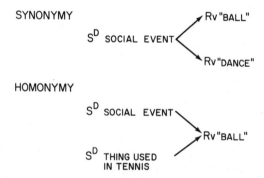

Synonymy is the result of an extended reinforcement history, but it doesn't increase the precision of the discriminations of either the speaker or the hearer. Using a synonym clarifies matters by tapping the hearer's reinforcement history. But, the hearer and the speaker must have similar reinforcement histories if synonyms are to be helpful. The speaker who uses synonyms has had several reinforcement histories and goes through their products (tacts) until he finds one that serves as a discriminative stimulus for his hearer. Homonymy just leads to less discrimination on the hearer's part. Prolonged additional tacting is needed, and reinforced, so as to straighten it out. Some verbal communities are not willing to put up with all of this, and therefore Spanish speakers have relatively few homonyms.

THE SIZE OF THE RESPONSE IN TACTING

Earlier we said that the size of the response unit must be left open or flexible because different variables control responses of different sizes. We can examine various examples of tacts to see this variability.

Much tacting occurs with single units that correspond to the lexical words. For example, S^D object-Rv "shirt"; S^D property-Rv "white." If we change some part of the discriminative stimulus, it tends to show up as a single word change.

Some seemingly unbreakable word chains occur in tacts:

S^D	Rv
Spotless	Clean as a whistle
Basic ingredient	Nitty-gritty, warp and woof
Disorder	Helter-skelter
Correct	In apple-pie order

Here are some proper names that fill the bill: George Washington Bridge, Chicago Transit Authority, Harvard University. And, there are some multi-word Rv's of tacts that seem to be idiosyncratic. For example, a man I know says, "as busted as the Ten Commandments" and "as slick as a greased pig"; and another man I know says, "the hottest thing since sliced bread." Each is a unit because it always appears this way and never appears any other way.

Certain tacts occur with Rv's at a level below that of words. These fragments of words never occur without something else on the response side. Generally these fragments are what have traditionally been called roots. For example, if the discriminative stimulus is part of the total stimulus situation, "super" is likely to be part of the response, as in *super-structure, supervisor, superordinate*. If the stimulus situation includes an ongoing action, the Rv "ing" is likely to show up, as in *speaking, walking, sitting*. If the discriminative stimulus includes something below or lesser than something else, the Rv "sub" is likely to appear, as in *subordinate, subbasement, subthreshold*. These are all familiar from junior high school English class. However, many very fragmentary roots are not even syllables. The etymologies at the subsyllable fragment level are somewhat unexpected and are not well established in traditional accounts of language.

Here is an example from Skinner. If the discriminative stimulus contains emanation from a point source, the Rv is likely to be "sp," as in *spring, splash, spew, splay, splat, sprinkle, sparkle, spray, spangle, speak, sputter, splutter, spout.* Some other examples, which come from Bloomfield and MacCorquodale, are the following: If the discriminative stimulus is a nose, the Rv is likely to be "sn," as in *snout, snore, snooze, snuff, sniff, sniffle, sneeze, sneer.* If the discriminative stimulus is smooth and wet, the Rv is likely to be "sl," as in *slime, slush, slop, slobber, slip, slide, slither.* If the discriminative stimulus is diminutiveness, the Rv is likely to be the "short *i*" sound, as in the following: slot-*slit*, bang-*bing*, snap-*snip*, tang-*ting*, snuff-*sniff*, yap-*yip*. You can do this too. If you go through your dictionary, I think that you will be convinced that if the discriminative stimulus is long, slender, and twisting, the Rv "sk" is likely to appear; that if the stimulus has elements of attack, destruction, or reduction, the Rv "sm" is likely; and if the stimulus situation has elements that are smooth and flat, the Rv "pla" is probable.

This can lead to all sorts of fun word games, but there is a serious point to it. Namely, the speaker in certain situations is likely to make certain kinds of sounds because the discriminative stimuli present may strengthen a certain sound fragment on the basis of tact operants that occurred previously in old situations and were reinforced. Furthermore, the hearer is likely to reinforce these fragmentary response tacts because they "sound right" to him; they do so for the same reasons that the speaker is inclined to emit them. Sometimes an argument is made that these subsyllable sounds are onomatopoeic (sound like the discriminative stimuli). But, cross-cultural investigation dispatches such a claim easily; "sl" does not sound smooth and wet to a Frenchman. Here are some English words and their French translations:

Slake	Étancher
Sleek	Lisse, luisant, poli
Slime	Vase, bave
Slush	Boue, fange
Slob	Vase, limon
Slop	Lavasse
Slobber	Baver
Slip	Glisser
Slide	Glisser
Slither	Glisser, ramper (what a snake does), onduler
Sleet	Neige à moitié fondue
Slosh	Flanquer un coup à

Slug	Limace
Sluice	Ecluse, bonde
Slick	Adroit, en bon ordre
Slink	S'esquiver, se dérober
Slog	Cogner dur
Slough	Fondrière
Sludge	Boue, vase, cambouis

Fragmentary tacting may sometimes be seen occurring in the utterance of a kind of neologism called *portmanteau words*. The next illustration shows two examples of this. The first comes from Lewis Carroll, who was an expert at making them up. He was the one who gave them the name

$$S^D \text{ FURIOUS}$$
$$+ \quad\quad\quad\quad \longrightarrow Rv \text{ "FRUMIOUS"}$$
$$S^D \text{ FUMING}$$

$$S^D \text{ IMPLICATIONS}$$
$$+ \quad\quad\quad\quad \longrightarrow Rv \text{ "IMPLIFICATIONS"}$$
$$S^D \text{ RAMIFICATIONS}$$

portmanteau words because, as he said, they are like a flexible suitcase; you can get it all into one. Here we have new words explicitly composed of fragments of responses to old situations; the component Rv's and their discriminative stimuli are, according to Carroll, those depicted here. In many cases, the maker of a neologism knows what the component tacts are; in a few cases, he doesn't. What this does suggest, however, is that just about all new words are composed of components of old ones.

ABSTRACTIONS

This is somewhat elusive to some people because it is so contrary to our usual view on these matters, but if you bear with me and go over it again, I think you will see that it is coherent, and almost necessarily true. Earlier we considered tacts that named discriminative stimuli that are single isolated properties of objects and said that we would call these abstractions. Several aspects of that kind of behavior are of considerable importance.

If we want to condition an abstraction of tacting Rv "red" to redness as such, we have an interesting engineering problem, because whenever the Rv "red" is followed by reinforcement, something else other than redness is also present. Even though the discriminative stimulus red is a single isolated property of objects, it is almost never physically isolatable. Hence, red occurs in the presence of other discriminative stimuli, such as ball, book, sweater, cherry, and fire engine. So, these other discriminative stimuli always get some control over the Rv "red" with each reinforcement. It's just the metonymy case again. But this process seems to be taking the Rv "red" out of the control of the discriminative stimulus redness as such.

Stimulus control is sharpened and narrowed to redness as such, because it is the only property that is always present on reinforced occurrences of the Rv "red." The number of reinforcements for that tact is always greater than the number for any other interfering tact, so the tact of the discriminative stimulus redness—Rv "red"—is strongest of all.

There are always nonred occurrences of the other discriminative stimuli, such as silver barns, blue balls, yellow books, and green cherries. If by metonymy the wrong properties came to control the Rv "red," and it were evoked in the absence of the discriminative stimulus redness, it would not be followed by reinforcement (extinction). Therefore, the competing tacts would be weakened. So, finally, by a process of differential reinforcement and extinction, only one discriminative stimulus survives to exert a controlling relation over the Rv. Thus the discriminative stimulus redness and the Rv "red" covary and do so indifferently with respect to other aspects of the environment or the speaker's state. The Rv "red" then tells the hearer that the discriminative stimulus redness occurs somewhere in the speaker's environment, but it tells him nothing more; it could be any red thing.

This example illustrates how a tact repertoire that is controlled by relevant abstract properties can be generated and maintained regardless of context. Our repertoires of abstractions are very useful; we employ them extensively when we need to tact with utmost discrimination, and they allow us to tact extensively when confronted with a highly novel stimulus situation. When confronted with a new object or event and a requirement of an exact description, we tact color, weight, contour, texture, length, spatial location, numerosity. Tacts of this sort constitute what has been considered the bedrock language of experience (sense data language). You can tact anything with it, with great specificity.

The other striking aspect of abstractions is somewhat surprising and tends to evoke a great deal of controversy. Part of the answers to the questions that we will consider here will require additional data, but here goes. Abstractions, that is, a response vocabulary that covaries with single isolated properties anywhere and in any other set of discriminative stimuli, seem to exist only in animals who have been conditioned by a verbal community. That is, such a repertoire occurs only because there is, or was, a reinforcement mediator who did what was necessary. That is one who maintained the contingency between reinforcement and a Rv emitted in the presence of a specific isolated property. A reinforcement mediator is necessary because nothing else in nature will do so.

Consider tacting red. There is no response—conventional or otherwise, reflex, or ingestive—that nature will automatically or systematically reinforce in the presence of redness and extinguish otherwise. Therefore, wild (feral) animals, including men (if there are any), have no tact repertoire for such states of the environment. Red berries may be ripe and green ones may cause vomiting, so the feral man may learn to discriminate between the two kinds of objects. That is, the man learns to eat the *red berries* and not eat the *green berries*. He learns to respond to the objects as a pigeon would, and not to their properties. A man who has the abstractions red and green will respond to the properties (colors) *as such* apart from the objects. But nature does not reinforce such responding. However, something like a tact would occur if he tried to eat all red objects—berries, fish, coral, the setting sun, the fire engine. It still wouldn't be a true tact, because the reinforcer is unconditioned and depends on deprivation. Hence, responses to inedible objects would quickly extinguish, thereby destroying the incipient discrimination of an isolated property.

It seems that the next curious step follows inexorably with the full force of deductive logic. If redness, as such, plays no role in an animal's behavior, there is no reason to say that he perceives it. "Sensation" is unaffected. The feral man sees *red berries* as different from *green berries*. But red is not seen as such, as literally a thing isolated from its objects. The linguists Hoijer and Whorf were among the first to make such arguments. This view is called LINGUISTIC RELATIVISM AND CLAIMS THAT VERBAL OR SOCIAL BEHAVIOR ORGANIZES EXPERIENCE, RATHER THAN THE OTHER WAY AROUND. Part of the argument is the claim that two cultures might do it different ways, or that one might leave out something. The linguists and anthropologists don't seem to have agreed on any definite assessment of the truth of these conclusions. All we can say is that according to the sort of analysis we have been developing here, it should be the case that some variant of linguistic relativism is true.

DO ANIMALS TACT?

We must distinguish between "tacting" in feral, wild, nonpet, nonlaboratory animals and "tacting" in specially trained ones. Pursuing this topic is a good way to get a heated argument from some biologists and linguists. But, if the defining properties of the tact are that (1) it is conditioned operant behavior comprising a conventional repertoire, and (2) it is exclusively stimulus controlled (objective, disinterested), then I seriously doubt that wild animals tact. Irrespective of the merits and implications of the work of Wenner, Johnson, and Frisch, all that stomping and twisting about which "tells" the other bees where the nectar is located is probably not operant (see the recent note by Davenport). The same is true of bird songs. These are emotional cries; they are respondent and hardly disinterested. They act, if anything, as unconditioned elicitors for the behavior of other birds. Dolphins *might* tact, though, because they are smart social animals. However, no one has cracked their code as yet, so we cannot be sure whether they really have a linguistic community or are like the rest of the wild animals with primarily unconditioned emotional cries. These latter animals don't tact because they have no conditioned generalized reinforcers with which to put operant behaviors solely under stimulus control.

Can animals be made to talk? Two major experiments attempting to answer this question have been recently done with chimpanzees, but neither has been reported in sufficient detail to provide definitive answers to the question. Washoe, the chimpanzee trained by R. Allan Gardner and Beatrice Gardner, mands in American sign language. Each time she made a sign for an object, they tended to give it to her. In the *New Yorker*, Emily Hahn wrote that Washoe's then current owner, W. B. Lemmon, called Washoe the greediest chimpanzee that he had ever come across. David Premack's Sarah used pieces of colored plastic as Rv's and does seem to have some abstractions that are transferable from situation to situation. But it is hard to see whether these will remain as disinterested Rv's, since she was fed for correct responses. I would venture to say that mands have definitely been taught to chimps, and that tacting may be teachable. It's very intriguing, but we need much more information before we can come to any firm conclusions as to whether the animals can be taught a full repertoire of nonvocal verbal behavior.

If it takes a man or a woman to teach a chimp or a child how to engage in verbal behavior, who taught the first man? Who was the first reinforcement mediator? I don't know; I wasn't there. It isn't necessary for us to know how men first learned to talk. Our problem is how they get to talk now and what keeps them going. Being so far removed from the necessary observations, any hypotheses I might now make would be merest speculations, but for the sake of completeness, here goes one. I suppose that talking got started by accidental reinforcement of operant-level babbling in children, who then reinforced their parents and thus got the whole thing going. Once talking started, generalization and discrimination could take effect and extend repertoires.

As I said, how talking got started isn't really the problem we are addressing, so I won't take my speculations further. The variables left for us to consider are all discriminative stimuli, but the operants they control are not called tacts for one reason or another, which will become clear in the remaining chapters.

6

audiences

In this chapter we concentrate on the other individual in the interlocking verbal operant paradigm. So far we have concentrated on the speaker, and to the extent that we have discussed the other person it has been with respect to what he has done after the speaker has said something. We now consider the functions of the second person prior to the onset of a speech episode.

DEFINITION AND PARADIGM

We seem to have several names for individual B in the following paradigm. We give him a different name for each different function that he performs. Generally we call him the hearer, but when he comes in after verbal behavior and reinforces A's operants, he is called a reinforcement mediator or member of the reinforcing community. Because he must normally be present before verbal behavior occurs in order to come in after it with a reinforcement, he gets a certain amount of behavior conditioned to himself. HE IS A STIMULUS, AND HE, AS A STIMULUS, IS PRESENT WHEN OR JUST BEFORE REINFORCED RESPONDING OCCURS. HE BECOMES, THEREFORE, AN ANTECEDENT CONTROLLING DISCRIMINATIVE STIMULUS AND IS IN THIS ROLE CALLED AN AUDIENCE. He seems to exert three principal kinds of control:

$$A: \quad Rv \longrightarrow S^r$$

$$B: \quad S^D \longrightarrow R$$

$$A: \quad S^D \text{ AND/OR} \longrightarrow Rv \longrightarrow S^r$$
$$DEP^{\underline{N}} + S^D_{AUD}$$

$$B: \quad \text{PERSON B} \quad S^D \longrightarrow R$$

(1) As a *sole sufficient discriminative stimulus,* his presence may account completely for what is said. (2) As a *supplementary variable,* he may affect audibility and perhaps other production effects, but not the content of what is said. (3) He may be a supplementary variable affecting which Rv is emitted, i.e., what is said. If several Rv's are possible, the usual supplementary strengthening process may go on. Some other variable makes a variety of Rv's likely, and the discriminative stimulus of the audience contributes more strength to one or two Rv's so that they get said. We do not define a special class of operants, like the classes of mands and tacts, for the *audience* because, even though it is a discriminative stimulus, it is nearly always a supplementary variable. That is, it almost always contributes to the probability of a Rv that is already likely for some other reason. Furthermore, the audience affects verbal behavior in such diverse ways that a single definition of an operant class for it would be clumsy, if at all possible. This summarizes our examination of the audience; the rest of this chapter works it out.

ADDRESS

ADDRESS OCCURS WHEN THE AUDIENCE IS SUFFICIENT, OR NEARLY SO, TO EVOKE THE Rv IN QUESTION. Examples of Rv's in address include *"John", "Your Honor", "Ladies and Gentlemen", "Sir", "Officer", "Your Majesty", "Your Grace", "Your Royal Highness", "Hey Doc".* The relation is very similar to the tact. But address is not tacting. Loosely, we may say that in address, as opposed to the usual tact, nothing is being named or described. Many discriminative stimuli are both tacted and addressed (that is, they are either talked about or talked to) with identical Rv's, such as the discriminative stimuli John, the ladies, and the gentlemen. But many are not. For example, *"Mr. President", "Your Honor",* and *"My very dear sir"* are not the Rv's of the usual sorts of tacts. They are the Rv's of addresses—and only of addresses. So, if the discriminative stimulus

John is tacted (S^D John $\longrightarrow$ Rv "John"), some other person receives this Rv and uses it as a discriminative stimulus. The other person may also be the speaker himself. But if the Rv "John" functions merely to gain John's attention or as a way to begin, it is part of an address. It has been claimed that address has something of the mand about it; perhaps attention is being manded. But, unlike pure or extended mands, address is very stimulus controlled, and it occurs in many situations in which it is already clear to the speaker that the hearer is paying attention. Therefore it seems best to leave it in a class by itself with its own proper name. No harm is done if it turns out to be a very impure mand.

AUDIBILITY AND THE AUDIENCE

WE WILL EXAMINE HOW THE AUDIENCE SOMETIMES ACTS AS A CAT-ALYST. IT PROMOTES OR TRIGGERS SPEECH BUT DOES NOT DETERMINE WHAT IS SAID. If the speaker "has something to say" due to other variables' (primary variables) being effective, whether it is said aloud is, to an important degree, controlled by the presence or absence of a hearer. This is because the probability of reinforcement is essentially zero without a hearer. Notice that I didn't say that people never talk without an audience; I just said that the likelihood of their doing so is negligible. In his role of catalyst, the discriminative stimulus audience is like a phone bell; he doesn't control what is said, but whether it is. The catalytic effect is merely supplementary. The presumption is, of course, that it can be shown that most audible speech occurs if an audience is present, and that presenting a silent person with an audience increases the likelihood that he will begin to speak. As I have said, in this instance the audience is responsible for a production effect of Rv forms already controlled by something else. There is no need to go into any more detail on that; it's simple enough. However, certain other kinds of supplementary strengthening exerted by the audience are related to the pure audibility effect, but not the same thing. These occur when the strengths of the primary and supplementary variables are seriously mismatched.

When a *weak primary variable* is present along with a strong audience discriminative stimulus, several classic situations occur. For example, the instructor calls on you in class and you have no verbal behavior readily available, or an employment interviewer asks you a question for which you have no answer. Those are big, salient discriminative stimuli; they grade, or they determine whether you get to eat. Another example occurs when you go to a party and the hostess introduces you to some distinguished-looking beautiful person and leaves you with the Rv "I have been wanting you two to meet; you will have lots to talk about, I'm sure." (Never mind what it says in Emily Post, don't ever do that to anyone.) What happens? Lots of odds and ends that are weakly controlled are forced out by the supplementary strengthening from the discriminative stimulus audience. In the social situation the resulting verbal behavior has been called "devices." One tacts the weather or mands information about books or movies. It gives each speaker something to do, and also an opportunity to reinforce the other for speaking.

Sometimes the *primary variables* are *strong* and the person present is a weak audience, as a discriminative stimulus. The audience is less effective as a discriminative stimulus if its properties depart too much from the reinforcing community that the speaker has experienced in the past. Sometimes the discriminative stimulus of an audience is sufficiently dissimilar to the stimulus in the presence of which Rv's have been reinforced so that generalized operant strength is low. For example, the microphone and television camera, as well as the dictating machine, are sufficiently dissimilar to the discriminative stimulus audience that many people cannot use them. But the same people could talk fluently to a group of people without any further primary variable manipulation. So, some call in a typist who doesn't take shorthand while they talk into the dictating machine. Or, a small group of people is specially imported for the making of television tapes.

Surprisingly, the people listening to a lecture are often a poor discriminative stimulus. There are many people there, and they look like reinforcement mediators. But their behavior often lacks audience (mediator, hearer) properties. They don't respond, because they don't have to. The speaker is *behaved to* as if he were an object. Everyone is eavesdropping, but no one is reinforcing; it is all left to someone else. Often this occurs because the people there are not disposed to reinforce in any case. Experienced speakers then talk to the corners of the room, or to the clock on the back wall. They find surrogates, like the writer who learned to talk to his bathrobe. Also, experienced speakers learn to ignore the group and talk to a few people in it—the nodders and the smilers. They are the ones who either keep you on a topic or move you along (they, at least, behave *like* reinforcement mediators). The group of people that has been spoken to before is known to be "easier to talk to" because it becomes an effective discriminative stimulus through those occasional social reinforcers. But some members of the lecture audience are dangerous discriminative stimuli. You have to avoid talking to your friends, because your output may become too colloquial or intimate.

Professional writers pose something of a problem for this account. They do not seem to have any audience present when they are doing the writing. But, it is usually the case that they talk, if only very covertly, before or as they write. Many professional writers develop *surrogate audiences* by the use of special rituals in their writing. Professor Skinner, for one, has a special environment set up to provide discriminative stimuli to function principally as an audience and supplementarily strengthen that verbal behavior of his that is controlled by other primary variables. He has a special room in the basement of his house, which always has the same furniture, and to which he goes at the same time each day. Some professional writers have to use the same sweater or bedroom slippers or cap. It is all very routine. Anthony Trollope, the Victorian novelist, was awakened early every morning by his servant, so that by 5:30 A.M. he sat fully dressed at his desk in his study and opened his watch. Whereupon he wrote for a couple of hours, closed his watch, left his desk and study, and went off to begin his day as a British postmaster. It was a way of creating a set of strong discriminative stimuli for an "audibility effect," and it did produce a lot of supplementary strengthening of his verbal behavior—at least sixty books' worth.

Most of us don't have to go to these extremes, but we sometimes do use the same sorts of arrangements of discriminative stimuli to provide supplementary strengthening. The casual letter writer looks at "Dear Delilah's" picture while writing to her. For some people, that is the only way the letter can be written. Some sort of surrogate audience is necessary. The professional writer's surrogates are just as powerful; if he doesn't sit at his desk, or look at his watch, or wear his old baseball cap, he cannot write anything, no matter how much he "has to say" or is "inspired." Of course, the other side of the coin is very true. If primary variables are strong, even a weak discriminative stimulus audience will not stop speaking from occurring. The verbal behavior may be directed to the cat, the table, strangers, or no one at all, like that of the man who roamed the streets of downtown Minneapolis in the 1960s reciting the failures and ancestries of the Minnesota Twins baseball team. He was psychotic, but that's not why he did what he did; he did it because his primary variables were strong, and he carried them around with him. We will have to wait until we consider covert behavior before we can fully understand what his primary variables were.

It is appropriate to ask the following question, if the discriminative stimulus audience affects the audibility dimension of verbal behavior, where is the verbal behavior that is strong for other reasons but does not occur aloud because of the lack of a strong audience? That is, what are its physical dimensions and where do I measure them? Either or both of two answers apply. First, such verbal behavior may remain merely *more probable* at the moment. There may be an increased tendency or disposition for the behavior to occur, even though it does not in fact occur. Such an increased disposition *is testable*. The test is to present a supplementary variable, that is, create an audience as a supplementary discriminative stimulus and determine whether the speaker speaks as predicted, whether he says what you would have predicted him to say on the basis of knowing the primary variables affecting him. For example, we could present a food-deprived subject with an audience who has in the past fed him and see if the subject mands food.

Second, the verbal behavior may be COVERT. SOME, OR ALL, OF THE SAME MUSCLES MAY MOVE BUT MAY DO SO WITH VERY SMALL AMPLITUDES. THE AMPLITUDES OF THE MOVEMENTS MAY BE SO SMALL THAT SUCH MOVEMENTS CAN BE DETECTED ONLY BY ELECTRONIC AMPLIFICATION. And some movements, such as those involved in phonation, may drop out entirely. Muscle recordings have been made by many people (see the books by McGuigan and Schoonover and by McGuigan), and the muscle-produced movements are found where they are predicted to be. Thus our account is in good shape. Both processes probably happen, and neither is inconsistent with our natural science restrictions.

AUDIENCES AS RESPONSE SELECTORS

Given the situation shown in the upper part of the next illustration, where a primary variable controls several different Rv's with about equal strengths, only one Rv occurs. Sometimes, surprisingly, the weakest of the lot is the one that appears. Why is this? The answer seems to be given paradigmatically in the lower part of the illustration. The audience may act as a supplementary variable to strengthen momentarily one of the alternative operants available.

PROBLEM:

PRIMAY VARIABLE $\longrightarrow$ Rv_1 Rv_2 Rv_3 Rv_4 Rv_5

SOLUTION:

PRIMARY VARIABLE + S^D AUDIENCE $\longrightarrow$ Rv_1 Rv_2 Rv_3 Rv_4 Rv_5

$Rv_4 \longrightarrow Pr(Rv_4) \uparrow$ AND Rv GETS SAID

We can carry this analysis forward in somewhat greater detail. In the past, different subaudiences have differentially reinforced the speaker for emitting different Rv's to the same situation. THESE AUDIENCES, AS DISCRIMINATIVE STIMULI, BY BEING DIFFERENTIALLY PRESENT ON DIFFERENT REIN-

FORCEMENT OCCASIONS GET SOME CONTROL OVER THE Rv's PREFERENTIALLY REINFORCED BY THEM. THUS THEY BECOME DISCRIMINATED AUDIENCES AND CONTROL DIFFERENT RESPONSES. Remember the difference in tacting for the scientific audience and tacting for the literary audience; one wants to be told that a man is a "Scrooge," and the other wants to know his scores on a personality test. The scientist can be a member of both audiences, and tact to both. Which operants are momentarily stronger may be determined by which audience is present at the moment. Notice that this does not say or imply that the speaker "chooses his words" to suit his audience. He rarely had time to "pick them out," and he doesn't seem to be doing anything other than talking. He doesn't seem to be choosing or deciding or picking his words. The audience determines the words for him. He is just a place where variables come together and interact to produce responses; he is not a variable himself.

Sometimes the response selection powers of the audience may be sufficient to determine whether anything at all gets said. The next illustration depicts several examples of this. In the first case the presence of an audience will add to the Pr (Rv) so that something gets said, such as "May I have a hot dog." If there were no audience, there isn't much chance that the Rv would occur. Also, one audience, the fraternity brother, may supplement

$$DEP^N$$
$$+ \longrightarrow Rv \text{ "MAY I HAVE A HOT DOG"}$$
$$S^D_{AUD}$$
$$\text{(COOK)} \qquad Pr(Rv \text{ WITHOUT } S^D) \text{ IS VERY LOW}$$

$$S^D \text{ WELL-ENDOWED GIRL} \longrightarrow Rv \text{ "WOW!"}$$
$$+$$
$$S^D_{AUD}$$
$$\text{(FRATERNITY BROTHER)}$$

$$S^D \text{ SAME GIRL}$$
$$+$$
$$S^D_{AUD \text{ (MINISTER'S WIFE)}} \longrightarrow \text{NO OVERT } Rv$$

the strength of Rv's that tact the speaker's appreciation of the girl, whereas the other audience, the minister's wife, may reduce the Pr (Rv) to zero. We say, colloquially, that different audiences have different taboos and different enthusiasms. With some, if you make the wrong response, not only do you not get reinforced, you get punished. Some audiences are sufficiently aversive so that they may inhibit almost all the speaker's Rv's, or some extensive parts of his response repertoire.

Most importantly, the audience often determines which one of the several possible Rv's controlled by the primary variables actually gets said. There are six categories which have received names, but the same dynamic processes operate in all of them.

Bilingualism provides the clearest example, perhaps because of the extremeness of the changes in the response repertoire. The completely bilingual person has at least two Rv's per discriminative stimulus for which he has any tacts at all. If you change his audience you immediately change the whole repertoire. Translators tell us that there is no one-to-one correspondence between words of one language and those of another. That doesn't matter for our purposes. Remember that the size of the Rv is flexible here and rarely corresponds to lexical words. Analysis of bilingual people can be interesting from a personality standpoint. One of the oldest analyses was done by Hale in 1846 and has been extensively quoted by Jespersen and De Laguna. The writing is so entertaining that the work should be quoted rather than paraphrased:

> A very singular phenomenon in philology is the trade-language, or, as it is generally called, the Jargon, in use on the Northwest Coast, and in the Oregon Territory. The circumstances to which it owes its origin are probably as follows: When the British and American trading-ships first appeared on the coast, about sixty years ago, they found there many tribes speaking distinct languages. Had it chanced that any one of these had been of easy acquisition, and very generally diffused, like the Chippeway among the eastern tribes, the Malay in the Indian Archipelago, and the Italian in the Mediterranean, it would no doubt have been adopted as the medium of communication . . . Unfortunately, all these languages,—the Nootka, Nasquale, Tshinuk, Tsihalish, &c.—were alike harsh in pronunciation, complex in structure, and spoken over a very limited space. The foreigners, therefore, took no pains to become acquainted with any of them. But as the harbour of Nootka was, at that time, the headquarters or principal depot of the trade, it was necessarily the case that some words of the dialect there spoken became known to the traders, and that the Indians, on the other hand, were made familiar with a few English words. These, with the assistance of signs, were sufficient for the slight intercourse that was then maintained. Afterwards, the traders began to frequent the Columbia River, and naturally attempted to communicate with the natives there by means of the words which they had found intelligible at Nootka. The Chinooks, who are quick at catching sounds, soon acquired these words both in Nootka and English, and we find that they were in use among them as early as the visit of Lewis and Clarke, in 1804.
>
>   . . . it was soon found that the scanty list of nouns, verbs, and adjectives, then in use, was not sufficient for the purposes of the more constant and general intercourse that began to take place. A real language, complete in all its parts, however limited in extent, was required; and it was formed by drawing upon the Tshinuk for such words as were necessary . . . Having appropriated these, and a few other words of the same language, the "Jargon" assumed a

regular shape, and became of great service as a medium of communication;—for it is remarkable that for many years no foreigner learned the proper Tshinuk sufficiently well to be of use as an interpreter.

But the new language received additions from other sources. The Canadian **voyageurs**, as they were called, who enlisted in the service of the American and British fur companies, were brought more closely in contact with the Indians than any others of the foreigners. They did not merely trade, they travelled, hunted, ate, and in short lived with them on terms of familiarity. The consequence was, that several words of the French language were added to the slender stock of the Jargon . . . All the words thus brought together and combined in this singularly constructed speech are about two hundred fifty in number . . .

It may seem at first sight incomprehensible that a language, if such it may be called, composed of so few words, thus inartificially combined, should be extensively used as the sole medium of intercommunication among many thousand individuals. Various circumstances are, however, to be borne in mind, in estimating its value as such a medium. In the first place, a good deal is expressed by the tone of voice, the look, and gesture of the speaker. The Indians . . . are very sparing of their gesticulations. No languages, probably, require less assistance from this source than theirs. Every circumstance and qualification of their ideas is expressed in their speech with a minuteness which to those accustomed to the languages of Europe appears exaggerated and idle,—as much so as the forms of the German and Latin may seem to the Chinese. We frequently had occasion to observe the sudden changes produced when a party of natives, who had been conversing in their own tongue, were joined by a foreigner, with whom it was necessary to speak in the Jargon. The countenances which before had been grave, stolid, and inexpressive, were instantly lighted up with animation; the low, monotonous tone became lively and modulated; every feature was active; the head, the arms, and the whole body were in motion, and every look and gesture became instinct with meaning.

Interestingly, these shifts in personality will show up in responses to standardized personality tests. Ervin has found that French-English bilinguals will differ in their responses to the same Thematic Apperception Test (TAT) cards, depending upon whether they respond in French or English. When speaking English, bilingual women showed a greater need for achievement than when speaking French. Whereas when French was spoken, withdrawal, autonomy, and verbal aggressiveness toward peers were shown.

Variants of bilingualism occur in all of us, because we all are bilingual to some extent. Some of the best examples of bilingualism within a single language community also come from studies of speakers of Native American languages. Sapir studied the speech of the Yana tribe of northern California. He found that although there are no genders in the Yana language, as there are in the Romance languages for example, there are verb stems that apply exclusively to activities of males or of females. There are also special verbs for abnormal appearance, but these verbs take different forms when referring to males as opposed to females. But, more importantly, the male forms are used only by males while talking to males, whereas female forms are used by females while talking to either males or females, and by males while talking to females. However, if a female quotes a male who used the male forms, then the female will use the male forms in her quotation.

Sapir also studied the language of the Nootka tribe of Alberni Canal, Vancouver Island. The Nootka speakers add special suffixes and/or meaningless consonant forms to verbs. They will add a particular set of forms depending upon the referent of the speech. One set is added for children, another for fat people, another for very short adults, another for those suffering from some defect of the eye, another for hunchbacks, another for those that are lame, another for left-handed persons, and another for circumcised males.

Special audiences exist for all of us. *Cant* and *jargon* are the special vocabularies of professional trades. Practitioners speak to one another differently than they do when speaking with clients. One clinical psychologist may say to another, "Jones is a seven, nine," thereby tacting Jones's primary peaks on a personality test and hence certain aspects of his personality. Jargon is perfectly good and useful, no matter what the freshman composition instructors say. They didn't realize it, but they were just trying to get you to use *their* jargon most of the time. Jargons are specially invented, not out of sloppiness, but because of expertise; they reflect the speaker's ability to make fine discriminations and to tact things that the layman cannot. If you can learn them, especially Skinner's, good for you. *Argot* used to be the thieves' cant or jargon. More about that very shortly.

Slang is the Rv repertoire of one's peer group. It shifts rapidly and is very faddish. It is the language of the "now" generation, even though it recycles. It is always auxiliary to the main repertoire, and it makes everyone a bilingual and, to a certain extent, part of the peer group. The *little languages* have technically been called *hypocorism*. One talks baby talk to babies and to very intimate adults. Hypocorism is filled with mangled pronunciations, and much of the standard repertoire is left out. Various *twin languages* (secret languages used by sibling twins) belong in this class, as do any sorts of *private languages* (special languages used by a social crowd or a pair of lovers).

Audiences control *special production effects.* We speak loudly to the audience that wears a hearing aid, and slowly and sometimes too loudly to the audience that looks foreign. Lieutenant Bush, in C. S. Forester's *Hornblower* series, used to have a special repertoire for Spanish-speaking audiences: He ended each Rv with "oh" in the belief that it would make him understood. This is carried further by most of us who have special repertoires for animals. We say "shoo" when the discriminative stimulus is a fly, but "scat" when it is a cat. Frederick the Great provides us with the best example. He claimed to speak French to the diplomats, Spanish to the clergy, Italian to the ladies, and German to his dogs.

MULTIPLE AND CONCURRENT AUDIENCES

Because we speak differently to different audiences, if two sub-audiences are concurrently present, some special effects are possible. A lot of verbal play may occur. *Secret languages* may occur. These allow the speaker to bypass one audience completely. *Argot* was the thieves' cant or jargon during the seventeenth and eighteenth centuries. It was a way of planning a crime in the presence of the victim without alerting him. We do this today; we spell when children are present. My grandparents would speak Russian when discussing whether to allow my father and his brother to go to the movies.

In *irony* verbal behavior is ambiguous; both audiences respond to it but do so differently. It depends on some disposition of one part of the audience to respond one way, while the other, having a somewhat different reinforcement history, is likely to respond otherwise. The following figure illustrates what is going on. For the speaker, either of the two discriminative stimuli is sufficient as a controlling variable. Because of his previous role as

a reinforcement mediator, he is able to discriminate the controlling relations. It becomes special fun when one part of the audience discriminates only one of the controlling relations, and the other part discriminates both. An aspiring author submitted his new novel as a late entry in a famous prize competition and received a letter from one of the judges, who sent carbons to the others, which read: "Thank you for your entry. I shall waste no time in reading your new book." I overheard one professor stop another, who was carrying a copy of the book review magazine *Contemporary Psychology*, and say, "I'm looking for a good book on cognitive psychology." The carrier replied, "Look no further." When both audiences are in the same skin, these are called *double entendres*.

SHAPING BY THE AUDIENCE:
A PERSONALITY EFFECT

I have argued that the audience exerts fairly strong but often subtle effects upon the immediate momentary behavior of a speaker. It can also shape a lot of verbal behavior, that is, create new Rv's or increase the probability of some Rv's. It does this surprisingly rapidly, considering that it is only a supplementary variable. This effect has been overlooked or denied. Some psychotherapists claim that they serve as audiences in the catalyst sense only when they are performing their therapeutic roles. It is claimed that the job of the therapist is to become a person in whose presence any verbal behavior may audibly occur. But therapists probably do a lot of shaping (differential reinforcement of successive approximations to the desired response) on the spot. There is a long history of finding evidence for the interviewer's point of view in protocols (recall the experiment by Hildum and Brown). Remember that Freud's hysterical ladies all claimed to have been sexually assaulted when they were children. It was part of his theory at the time. How could this have happened? A few nods, smiles, "oh's," "really's," "can you tell me more about that's," and "um-hmm's" at accidentally appropriate places could do the trick. Dr. Estes, whose experiments I described on pages 47-48 did much the same thing with her clock. And of course, Greenspoon shaped plural nouns with his "mmm-hmm." There is a huge literature on this, which I don't want to go into here. If you are interested, you might look at the chapter by Holz and Azrin in the book edited by Honig, which is listed in the References. Robert Rosenthal's book on experimenter effects in psychology also contains some information on these processes.

ONE'S SELF AS ONE'S AUDIENCE

We have considered the speaker as a self-mander and a self-tacter. We aren't very durable reinforcement mediators for ourselves, but if we have external reinforcement mediators to keep our verbal behavior strong, we are an excellent audience for ourselves. We are the ones to whom we do the most talking. After all, I am always *available* to me. I have privileged access to covert verbal behavior. I may, however, address myself overtly if there is a lot of background noise, or the problem is a hard one, or there is no one else about. I further have the advantage that I can be spoken to covertly, thus avoiding aversive stimulation which might arise from my overt behavior. I, as listener, have the same response repertoire as speaker; I "know all the words." It is a way of hearing interesting things sometimes. Occasionally, verbal behavior that never appeared before appears in talking to one's self. If I want to find out what I know, I don't inspect my ideas; I start talking and listen to myself. If I want to find a new solution to a problem, I start talking about it, and sometimes, if I talk long enough, I hear something new, which may serve as a discriminative stimulus for other behavior which will be reinforced. Finally, and this is only "introspective," the self is a very tolerant hearer. Rv forms seem different. Much is omitted, mostly what will later be discussed as autoclitic verbal behavior. Speech to one's self is often very *un*grammatical in the interests of speed. We must brood about this for a while, but we will have to save it for a later chapter.

7

echoics

DEFINITION AND PARADIGM

AN ECHOIC IS A VERBAL OPERANT WHOSE CONTROLLING VARIABLE IS ANOTHER SPEAKER'S VERBAL BEHAVIOR, AND WHOSE Rv'S ACOUSTIC PROPERTIES, IF AUDIBLE, REPRODUCE THE STIMULUS. The paradigm is given in the following illustration. Speaker B gets things going by being affected by some primary variable (P.V.), then speaking and thus providing the stimulation for Speaker A. It is A who does the echoing. This indicates that

$$S^D \text{"DOG"} \longrightarrow Rv \text{ "DOG"}$$

A:
(ECHOER)

B: P.V. $\longrightarrow$ Rv "DOG"

sometimes a speaker, such as A, says something simply because he just heard someone else say it. Thus, in our notational system the discriminative stimulus is put in quotes to indicate that it is itself verbal behavior or such behavior's acoustic product.

Generally, but not always, the echoic response reproduces more than the "words" of the speaker who got things started. Production effects such as pitch, rate, and inflection may be echoed. These may be extremely important, or in some cases all that is echoed; for example, some people who live in the North and visit the South on a vacation return home with southern accents. If, for some reason, a respected and admired professor says "odd hoke" instead of "ad hoc," then all the graduate students in his seminar go around saying it that way, even though they know (?) better.

All of this is unusual; most behavior does not *reproduce* the stimulus that controls it. A man may echo when there is no behavior to imitate—he may echo the airplane or the coffee pot, or the tea kettle.

Furthermore, because echoics are operants, each speaker must learn how to echo, that is, these operants must be conditioned at some time. Echoing seems "natural" or unlearned somehow, but it is conditioned. It is not the case that if you can perform a response, you will therefore be able to do so immediately under imitative control. For example, you have the vocal equipment, and hence the capability, to say the French word *rue* correctly in Parisian French. But you could not imitate a Parisian. That is because you have no echoics for this response. They can be manufactured though; the next illustration shows how. If the reinforcement community detects a good acoustic match between the discriminative stimulus and the echoer's Rv,

then it reinforces. If you remember the conventional correspondence between the discriminative stimulus and Rv in the tact, and the reinforcement mediator's discrimination of that correspondence as the basis of reinforcement, then this will seem very familiar. It might, in fact, be argued that the echoic is a subspecies of tact. Because it has special properties, namely the discriminative stimulus being overheard speech and the Rv reproducing the discriminative stimulus, we keep it in a class by itself. The next illustration shows this last point paradigmatically. The reinforcements for tacting and echoing are mediated on very different bases at very different times—the echoic is a very early operant; tacts are taught later. The upper branch of the illustration shows a collection of tacts of a Rv that served as their discriminative stimulus. Notice that these do not reproduce the discriminative stimulus.

I want to be able to include in echoics covert Rv's which, if audible, would reproduce their controlling stimuli, because, to anticipate again, listening seems to be composed largely of covert echoics (more about that later). Putting in covert echoics causes no problems. If we can speak quietly when

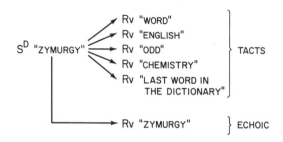

manding or tacting, we can speak quietly when echoing. So, the Rv's of echoics can sometimes be so quiet as to be inaudible, and all that is left is the kinesthetic feedback (proprioceptive stimulation) to the speaker. Hence, variations along the intensive dimension of audibility need not seriously disrupt our classificatory scheme or our use of it. Similarly, I have emphasized that the speech of some other individual serves as the discriminative stimulus in echoics. This is not to deny the existence of self-echoics, but most of what seems to be self-echoic verbal behavior is due to something else. Often "within speaker repetitiousness" occurs because the variable that made him say it the first time is still present; or he may repeat because he was reinforced, just as the pigeon does (the man at the party tells the same joke to everyone that night because "it went over well").

Echoics are composed of conditioned operants and are not the product of an instinct. I mention this only because some people seem to believe that echoic behavior is instinctive. There isn't a shred of evidence that indicates that there is an innate species specific disposition to echo verbal behavior. The best evidence for the *contrary* to the instinct proposition is that as children we can make sounds that we cannot echo as adults. The parrot or any other bird that instinctively echoes makes no sounds with his vocal apparatus that it cannot echo whether it be juvenile or adult. In misspeaking, we make sounds that we cannot echo. More importantly, any normal speaker can potentially emit any sound in any language. But he only echoes the sounds in the language that he either grew up in or learned to speak later when he received tuition in echoics. If echoism were instinctive, it would not be so selective as to limit itself to one language. If we want an example of instinctive behavior, we can look at the nesting goose. According to Konrad Lorenz, she rolls into her nest any object that is egg shaped, irrespective of its size or color or texture or weight. The egg-rolling *instinct* is not selective, but noninstinctive operant echoism is.

However odd or unusual, the echoic discriminative stimulus is a very potent variable. It has some surprising manifestations or powers. If instructed to, we, as proficient speakers, can echo. That is, we have echoic repertoires for some of the sounds that we can make. We can, under echoic control, emit Rv's that we have never emitted before and do so, moreover, without past histories of reinforcement or the presence of special primary variables. All that is required is our echoic repertoires and a reinforcement mediator who says, "Repeat after me. I, Stephen, do take . . ." Well, that's not so surprising. But we can, if "good manners" demand, mispronounce something so as not to offend, that is, say it in a way that is completely new for us. This is caused, not by "politeness," but by echoic dispositions. That is, we have been reinforced in the past for echoing the elements of the new stimulus.

ECHOISM IN CHILDREN

If we ask how echoics occur, the answer is that the reinforcement community reinforces some verbal behavior because it is echoic. The reasons why it does so are especially interesting and seem to change as the speaker gets older. We will therefore look at the reinforcement history for echoism in two stages.

An echoic vocabulary and echoic control over an infant's verbal behavior is, apparently, a practical necessity in teaching a child to talk. It is the first stage in which Rv's are explicitly reinforced by a mediator, that is, the first stage in which *mediated* reinforcements appear. To see this we will look at the chronology of learning to talk and see where the echoics show up.

Stage one is that of OPERANT LEVEL (OL) RESPONDING. THIS CORRESPONDS TO THE RAT'S "UNCONDITIONED" OR "SPONTANEOUS" BAR-PRESSES BEFORE SUCH RESPONSES EVER PRODUCE REINFORCEMENTS. IN THE VERBAL CASE THIS CONSISTS OF BABIES' BABBLING, UNCONDITIONED, UNDIFFERENTIATED, UNDISCRIMINATED Rv's. Children make noise. Each child does so because he is a human infant; he is genetically disposed to. This is where the genetic preprogramming comes in. Recall that verbal behavior is operant behavior; it is emitted and not elicited. Operants are created when responses are followed by reinforcements. The child's genetic constitution causes his nervous system to produce low probability, undifferentiated, undiscriminated behavior out of which operants are carved by reinforcement. So, operant-level verbal behavior consists of randomly occurring phones (sounds that can be heard as different). It can, and probably will, include all phonemes that occur in all languages, according to Jakobson and to Kaplan and Kaplan. As an infant, a person will say things he will claim that he is unable to echo later. There is, at least, no restriction of his babbling to the phonemes of his parents' language. Thus he doesn't inherit a French palate or a Bronx glottal stop.

Stage two consists of "ECHO-BABBLE" PRODUCED BY AUTOMATIC, NONMEDIATED REINFORCEMENT. THIS STAGE BEGINS ALMOST AT ONCE; THE BABBLE REPERTOIRE BECOMES REPETITIVE AND SHRINKS IN NUMBER AND

VARIETY OF SOUNDS TOWARD THOSE PHONEMES OF THE PARENTS' LANGUAGE. This comes about because the baby has been talked to in these sounds while being reinforced (fed, watered, dried, burped, tickled, rocked, patted, etc.). These sounds become conditioned reinforcers. Then, in babbling, when one of these sounds that he makes occurs, a Rv is "followed by" reinforcement immediately! It's automatic, and the rate goes up; the child does it again just like a bird pecking a key for food. The next illustration shows in an abbreviated notation what occurs, and it also explains the notation used. The first line shows the symbol for a Rv that is also a conditioned reinforcer (e.g., "good"); the second line shows the symbol for a Rv that is also a discriminative stimulus (e.g., "fire"); and the third and fourth lines show some combined notation that points to both functions carried out by a Rv. Finally, the last lines show the paradigm for the dynamics of the narrowed, repetitious echo-babble, where each response produces a sound that reinforces itself (S^r) and is also a stimulus (S^D) that causes the same R to recur, and the whole cycle goes off again and again and again. The process is automatic, but the reinforcing power of the Rv is not "intrinsic" or residing in

$$Rv : S^r$$

$$Rv : S^D$$

$$S^{r \cdot D}$$

$$Rv : S^{r \cdot D}$$

IN THE PAST: Rv "GOO" $\longrightarrow$ Rv "GOO"
                $+ S^r$ BOTTLE

SO LATER:

$$Rv : S^{r \cdot D} \longrightarrow Rv : S^{r \cdot D} \longrightarrow Rv : S^{r \cdot D}$$

FOR EXAMPLE:
    "GOO" $\longrightarrow$ "GOO" $\longrightarrow$ "GOO"

the words or phonemes as such. The reinforcing power got there through the actions of adults; it was conditioned, and so is the increase in the rate of babbling and the narrowing of its range.

Now we, and the infant, are ready for the explicitly tuitional phase of echoics. The child has a history of repeating some of what he hears, because he has conditioned himself to echo some sounds. Therefore, if the parent generates one of these sounds, the sound is forthcoming from the child, because the sound is already a discriminative stimulus with control over that Rv. This may seem odd, but consider it. The parents begin with "Say da da," "Say ma ma," "Say bow wow," and things of that sort. The child echoes *some* of it. At least he will sooner or later, and, most significantly, he will echo those parts that he has already echo-babbled. He may leave out the rest or substitute some other Rv's due to induction or generalization. No matter; the parent is "pleased" and reinforces, usually vigorously with attention and affection. So, the echoic is probably the child's first explicitly mediated operant. A whole echoic repertoire of these is explicitly formed by narrowing the child's Rv's to smaller classes of phonemes, creating phonemic chains, and putting these under auditory stimulus control.

There is a chronology to the development or evolution of the child's echoic vocabulary. It starts out with phonemes; in babbling, the unit may have been even smaller (phones). In early tuition, the child gets as stimuli morphemes or bigger units, all of which may be composed of several phonemes each. The child echoes those phonemes that he can. For example, one child was told to "say elephant" and responded with something that sounded like "efunt." No matter, she got reinforced. After a while new discriminative stimuli got echoic control over their corresponding Rv's, so that she could echo some of the previously missing phonemes. Irwin reports some other examples. One child's echoing of "milk" went through the stages of "meme," "mik mik," "milk." Another child, in echoing "please," started with "ble," then went through "pez," "pivez," and finally got to "please." Interestingly, when such new echoics appear they show up in all verbal situations containing that sound, at once. That's not surprising; it is indeed what we should expect. The discriminative stimuli were there all along; they hadn't previously had control, but once the control is achieved in one situation, whenever the discriminative stimulus appears in the speech of another person, the child now has an echoic for it. So, at some time it all gets there; all the phonemes of the parents' language are in the child's echoic repertoire.

At this time, still, the child cannot be said to "know what he is saying." He says "drop dead" because somebody else just did; he doesn't know that it *means* something. But once there is echoic control, the parent has a tremendous amount of power to shift control of the child's verbal behavior to other discriminative stimuli. The next illustration shows how this is done. By the same process that underlies metonymy, the child's tacts are

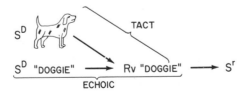

formed. The Rv of an echoic is passed along to other discriminative stimuli. One need not wait for the Rv "doggie" to occur in the presence of the animal; it would be a very long wait and the dog and the child might both die first. Notice that what occurs here does not fit the Pavlovian paradigm. The child's Rv is already under stimulus control, and it got that way through reinforcement. That is, he was reinforced in the past for echoing his mother. Also, for the metonymical extension of control to work, the mediator must reinforce the Rv in the presence of both discriminative stimuli—the Rv "doggie" which gets the child to say "doggie" as an echoic Rv, and the discriminative stimulus the animal itself. But this is easily arranged. The mother sees the dog and tacts "doggie," the child echoes the mother in the presence of the discriminative stimulus of the dog and gets reinforced, and the dog gains some control over the child's tongue. All sorts of naming can be taught this way, object class names and property names as well as proper names.

ECHOISM IN ADULTS

There seems no reason to doubt the existence of the tendency to echo and the continuing availability of the echoic vocabulary into adulthood. Echoics evidently continue to be formed after we have finished learning how to talk. I think that this is because echoism is maintained (reinforced) by other contingencies which persist throughout the life of the adult.

Speakers reinforce echoism on the part of hearers; it indicates *attention*. For example, a man's wife interrupts one of her monologues, which is beginning to be long enough to be a Sears catalog, to say, "you haven't been listening to a word I said . . . " So the husband replies, "I have too; you said . . . " This is the model. If the hearer echoes correctly, the speaker reinforces positively or withdraws aversive stimulation. Echoism is also indicative of *understanding* and *agreement*. If speaker A says, "It's a nice day"; speaker B is most likely to say, "Yes, it is indeed a nice day." This interchange is in large part echoic, B's echoics reinforce A's and set up a reinforcement for B in terms of A's next behavior. If B had said, "No, it is not a nice day at all," it would be partly echoic too, but it wouldn't be as reinforcing or as reinforceable. Attention and understanding are necessary preconditions to reinforcement for the echoed speaker. They reinforce the speaker whose behavior is echoed, so he reinforces the echoics.

Many people speak ill of echoics as a symptom of understanding; they charge that echoing is a test of "mere parroting," as if it were stupid to do it. What is so *mere* about being able to talk the way Einstein did? My advice to you is to parrot, at least at first. A circumlocution has a greater chance of being wrong. Parroting flatters the instructor; a circumlocution suggests that he could have said it better the first time. In many disciplines, especially those with precise subject matter, only echoics will do. And some fields are closed by convention. Spelling is no longer regarded as a field for creative work. Nor are you reinforced much for telling what eight times seven is "in your own words."

Echoics, furthermore, constitute easily available avoidance or escape operants; they terminate silences which usually are aversive. If I say to you, "Tell me the difference between mands and tacts," you may reply, "Well, the difference between mands and tacts is that a mand . . . " This gives the echoer time; it shows that he at least heard the question. It may also serve to stimulate further verbal behavior in the form of operants called intra-verbals. It gives the speaker something to say in the strong-audience-weak-primary-variable case.

SOME ODDS AND ENDS

To the extent that animals vocally "talk," they do so in an echoic fashion. Parrots, myna birds, and crows echo; the bird doesn't want the cracker. It isn't a mand; if you gave it a saltine, it wouldn't eat it. Dolphins echo. This, amazingly, may be conditioned by their trainers. It seems that neither the dolphins nor the trainers have generated metonymical extension to other stimuli. Dolphin echoics are hard to work with because they occur at high speed and at very high frequencies. Often they have to be slowed down with a tape recorder to be detected as echoism.

Skinner's analysis of verbal behavior does not entirely rule out the possibility of self-echoics; however, it does not seem that they are very frequent or important. We saw that repetitious verbal behavior in adults is more likely to be due to other variables. One variable may be the continued presence of the primary variable which made the speaker emit that Rv in the first place, such as "No, no, no" if it doesn't stop; "Ouch, ouch, ouch" if it still hurts; "Come in, come in" if they just stand there. Or, if something "goes over well," that is, gets reinforcement, it is likely to be repeated, as is done by the man who retells the punch line again after people have just laughed at his joke. Also, and perhaps more importantly, self-echoics are likely to be punished if they occur, for example, "I heard you the first time; I'm not deaf." Which is functionally: I'll reinforce *you* for echoing *me*, but don't repeat *yourself*. Even so, some repetitious verbal behavior may be self-echoic, but it usually occurs in children's speech, if at all. Perhaps a child sits alone in a room and says, "I good boy; I good boy; I good boy."

HEARING AND ECHOICS

What we have considered is important enough, that is, echoics play a major role in learning to talk and in showing interest, agreement, and understanding. But another whole function is suggested. The principal activity of the hearer as a *listener* (what he is doing as the speaker speaks, but not as a reinforcement mediator or as a discriminative stimulus) is to engage in *covert echoics* (small amplitude). This proposition is a consequence of our general stimulus-response position with respect to verbal behavior. In this view, listening, like any other "perceptual" activity is not just passive absorption. Hearing is not something that ends when "messages" or "bits of information" go from the ears to the brain. Hearing is an activity; conditioned operant behavior which is probably heavily echoic; the hearer talks along with the speaker. James J. Jenkins once said that this was the theory that claimed that "you hear with your tongue." This is sometimes called the motor theory of speech perception. It has several variants and proponents. We will see where ours takes us later on in this book.

8

textuals

DEFINITION AND PARADIGM

A TEXTUAL IS A VERBAL OPERANT WHOSE CONTROLLING VARI-
ABLE IS WRITING OR PRINTING, AND WHOSE Rv IS FUNCTIONALLY EQUIVALENT
TO THE PROPER NAME OF THE STIMULUS. The following illustration introduces
some examples of textuals and some paradigmatic conventions. When the
stimulus is a text (writing or printing), we put it on a piece of paper, that is,
draw the box around it, in our paradigmatic notation. Such things as the
semicolon, hyphen, dash, comma, and apostrophe are not discriminative

$$S^D \boxed{\text{HAT}} \longrightarrow \text{Rv "HAT"}$$

$$S^D \boxed{\text{C}} \longrightarrow \text{Rv "C"}$$

$$S^D \boxed{\text{\&}} \longrightarrow \text{Rv "AND"}$$

$$S^D \boxed{,\ldots} \longrightarrow \text{Rv " " [PAUSE]}$$

$$S^D \boxed{;} \boxed{--} \boxed{'}$$
$$\text{FOR TEXTUALS NOT } S^{D\prime}\text{s}$$

stimuli of textuals in this sense. They do not control any of the reader's
Rv's. I'll back off a little on this; the dash may be a textual discriminative

stimulus if it functions in the same way as three dots do, to generate a pause. There is no problem here; more than one person can have the proper name "Fred." So, more than one discriminative stimulus can have the proper name that is a pause in speech.

Stimulus and response units in textuals are surprisingly complex. Technically, ultimately when the speaker is well conditioned the stimulus unit is usually identified by the white spaces. The speaker responds to whatever is bounded by white spaces by naming that much, as in the lower part of the next illustration. He says "hat," not "h," "a," "t." If the letters

$$S^D \;\boxed{\text{H-A-T}} \longrightarrow Rv \text{ "H," "A," "T"}$$

$$S^D \;\boxed{\text{HAT}} \longrightarrow Rv \text{ "HAT"}$$

are separated by white spaces or by a special convention of dashes (which are named by pausing), the second type of response may occur. Other response units may be larger or smaller. If the stimulus within the white spaces is unfamiliar, we may give the names of its parts, as in reading "phonetically." Sometimes whole phrases are the response units, as when the minister reads his sermon aloud or when the president reads the State of the Union Address from a typewritten text: He looks down, and then goes on at some length.

Interestingly, the pauses in the spoken part of a stream of textuals bear little resemblance to those in the discriminative stimuli on the page. Illiterates just learning to read find the white spaces on the page somewhat disconcerting because they do not seem to covary with either silence or sound. They are, as we noted, lexical, textual, stimuli to the reader: "Name this much."

It may seem odd or forced to say that the Rv of a textual is "functionally the proper name of the discriminative stimulus." But technically this is correct; the Rv names and does not describe. The next figure illustrates this important difference paradigmatically. A book review, for example, is

THIS IS POSSIBLE:
$$S^D \;\boxed{\text{HAT}} \longrightarrow Rv \text{ "HAT"} \left.\right\} \begin{array}{l}\text{TEXTUAL}\\ \text{(NAMES)}\end{array}$$

BUT, SO ARE THESE:
$$S^D \;\boxed{\text{HAT}} \begin{array}{l} Rv \text{ "WORD"}\\ Rv \text{ "ENGLISH"}\\ Rv \text{ "SHORT"}\\ Rv \text{ "NOUN"}\\ Rv \text{ "MARK"}\end{array} \left.\right\} \begin{array}{l}\text{TACTS}\\ \text{(DESCRIBE)}\end{array}$$

governed by a text, but is not composed of textuals. Textuals do occur in quoting the book in the review. Rv's in word-association experiments that use mimeographed stimulus booklets are not textuals; they do not name the stimuli. Subjects tend to emit textual Rv's, but the experimenter instructs them not to record them, and to wait for what we will see in the next chapter are called intraverbals (the "associations"). Thus the Rv "A" is the *name* of a stimulus; it does not tell you that it is two lines and a crossbar, and so on. It is not tacting in our technical sense; it does not employ a descriptive vocabulary.

Like discriminative stimuli for proper naming, the stimuli for textuals have very narrow and precise controlling relationships. In proper names, if we generalize from one person or object to another which looks similar, we are wrong from start to finish. "George Washington Bridge" is not the name of the Golden Gate Bridge. Likewise, Rv "hat" is the name of only one text, and only one text has that Rv under stimulus control. But there are exceptions, just as in proper names. The next illustration gives two examples of textual ambiguities. Their proper naming counterparts are easy to

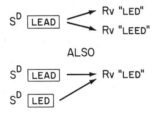

illustrate. What in the textual case are called *homographs* (upper part of the illustration) correspond to the person discriminative stimulus for which there are two Rv's, for example, "B. F. Skinner" or "Fred." The lower part of the illustration shows a *homophone*, a case where two discriminative stimuli properly control the same Rv. The personal proper-naming case is also easy to illustrate. The discriminative stimuli B. F. Skinner and F. S. Keller both control the Rv "Fred."

Notice that in the first case (homographs) the Rv's are very different, and that in the second case (homophones) the discriminative stimuli are very dissimilar. These cases are not due to extensive generalization, because, as in proper naming of people, similar discriminative stimuli for texts do not control similar Rv's. Just as two people who look alike do not have the same or similar names, two words that look alike do not necessarily control similar Rv's. The next illustration depicts several examples of cases following this rule. Because, even at the word level, generalization is risky, ultimately, in English, the whole word must be learned. This is probably due to our messy orthography. But all of this does not mean that a speaker is helpless when he first encounters a textual stimulus whose name he does not know. He can emit phonic Rv's to its component parts until something recognizable is said. It isn't necessarily the best way to learn new textuals. Orthography doesn't indicate stress, so the speaker may be misled.

EXAMPLES OF RISKY (NOT LIKELY TO BE REINFORCED) GENERALIZATIONS FROM TEXTUAL S^D's

GIVEN A PREVIOUS REINFORCEMENT HISTORY SUCH AS THIS	FOLLOWED BY A S^D SIMILAR TO ONE FOR WHICH Rv REINFORCED	THE WRONG Rv MAY OCCUR BECAUSE OF GENERALIZED S^D CONTROL FROM SIMILAR S^D, AND SUCH Rv's MAY GO UNREINFORCED
S^D [c] $\longrightarrow$ Rv "c" $\longrightarrow$ S^r	S^D [o] $\longrightarrow$	Rv "c" $\longrightarrow\!\!\!/\!\!\rightarrow$ S^r
S^D [SCOW] $\longrightarrow$ Rv "SCOW" $\longrightarrow$ S^r	S^D [COW] $\rightarrow$	Rv "SCOW" $\longrightarrow\!\!\!/\!\!\rightarrow$ S^r
S^D [THROUGH] $\longrightarrow$ Rv "THROUGH" $\longrightarrow$ S^r	S^D [ROUGH] $\rightarrow$	Rv "THROUGH" $\longrightarrow\!\!\!/\!\!\rightarrow$ S^r
S^D [CO-WORKER] $\rightarrow$ Rv "CO-WORKER" $\rightarrow$ S^r	S^D [COW] $\longrightarrow$	Rv "CO-WORKER" $\longrightarrow\!\!\!/\!\!\rightarrow$ S^r

In spite of the proper-name relationship between the discriminative stimulus and the Rv in the textual, textuals seem to be extremely strong operants, whereas discriminative stimulus control of personal proper names can be very weak. That is, we seem to forget people's names rather easily, but not so with the names of textual discriminative stimuli. For example, if the discriminative stimulus is the printed word *bear*, the first Rv seems inexorably determined; what you say is "bear," not "word" or "English" or "animal" or any other kind of tact or intraverbal Rv. Something always appears first, and it is the discriminative stimulus's proper name. This control is so strong and so precise that with it you can make hundreds of people say exactly the same thing at exactly the same time, as in responsive reading in church or singing from a score.

Not only do people never seem to forget how to read, once they are taught, textual control also makes them say things that they have never said before, or may never have heard either. If in reading one comes across a new word, one can say something. It may be the wrong name, but still it is verbal behavior (textual operants). One names the parts. For example, people say "literary" words that don't normally show up in speech, such as pshaw, ahem, umph, mulct, sesquipedalian. Finally, although reading from copy is the most obvious case, textual control is much more widespread. Words in commonly displayed texts, billboards and other signs, tend to show up in verbal behavior whose primary controlling variables are different. If you are careful, you can see that on a long automobile trip the topics of conversation seem to leap out of the roadside advertising.

REINFORCING TEXTUALS

Creation of textual repertoires in children is usually a more formal and organized process than the creation of any other operant repertoires, with the possible exception of some intraverbals. In the United States nowadays, parents establish mands, tacts, echoics, and audience control, but reading is largely left to the teachers in the schools. The functional dynamics of the process are depicted in the next illustration. We may recog-

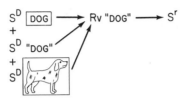

nize the process as one that capitalizes on metonymical extension and the gradual fading out of the discriminative stimuli which previously provided control of the Rv. The reinforcers are the ones that educators use, that is, generalized conditioned reinforcers. It is really very simple, and parents could do it at home if they wanted to; the child doesn't have to be a genius or have a high IQ. I guess that any normal child can be taught to read at age four. The major locus of the perennial controversy about how to teach reading lies in whether the discriminative stimuli should be words or letters. There are valid arguments on both sides. If the discriminative stimuli for explicitly taught textuals are whole words, then the child later has an impaired ability to deal with strange words; he hasn't much ability to piece things together phonically. If reading is taught by a *phonic* method, the child runs into problems because there isn't a one-to-one correspondence between orthography and pronunciation. There isn't really a lot for us to say about this controversy. All the different methods seem to work; the question is which is more efficient. Unfortunately, there doesn't seem to be any definite information on that.

Long after specific, on-the-spot, educational reinforcements have stopped, adults continue to respond textually to writing and printing. If you seat a man at a table in a restaurant, take his order, and leave him alone, he reads the label on the ketchup bottle. We must account for the amazing strength of textuals. One could argue that the man's teacher built his habits to such great strength that they would never be undone. That is, the teacher gave him such a big push that once he got going it was impossible for him to stop. This strains our understanding of behavior. If textuals are operants, they should be extinguishable, as are other operants, by means of nonreinforcement. If we can forget the names of our acquaintances, why can't we forget the names of marks on paper?

A more reasonable interpretation suggests that the answer to the preceding question is as follows. Textuals, like other operants, require reinforcement for their strength to be maintained. If the explicit tuitional reinforcements are no longer forthcoming for textual behavior, but the behavior still occurs with high probability, then some other reinforcement

contingencies must be effective in maintaining the strength of these operants. There are at least four major sources of added strength.

Our next illustration depicts the proposition that many texts tact; they
covary with stimuli and thus serve as discriminative stimuli that make other

S^D [BUS STOP] $\longrightarrow$ Rv: S^D "BUS STOP" $\longrightarrow$ R STAND $\longrightarrow$ S^r

S^D [CAFE] $\longrightarrow$ Rv: S^D "CAFE" $\longrightarrow$ R: S^D ENTER $\longrightarrow$ Rv "FOOD" $\longrightarrow$ S^r

S^D [ENTRANCE]

S^D [LOANS]

S^D [ONE WAY ⟩

S^D [GIVE THE MONEY TO THE MAN IN THE BLUE
SUIT AND THEN SELF-DESTRUCT]

reinforced behavior possible. People read for the same reason that they
listen to accurate tacting on the part of others. Tacts and textuals produce
discriminative stimuli which are useful to the hearer of them. They let him
respond in such a way that he gets reinforced.

Second, texts mand, and in so doing give advice. The last two texts in
the illustration do this. Again, generally, reinforcement for the reader is
guaranteed if his subsequent nonverbal behavior conventionally conforms
to the discriminative stimulus provided by the speaker under the control of
the text.

Third, texts are a source of intraverbals, that is, verbal operants under
the control of the speaker's own voice. (We will treat these in detail in the
next chapter.) Sometimes it is necessary to talk in a certain way; in my
classes I have to talk "like Skinner." That is easy; all I have to do is get a
text. It is the easiest, quickest, and surest way. Studying the text sets up
verbal chains which may be used (needed) later, that is, reinforced by a
mediator. These chains are subspecies of intraverbals. If, as in that situation, reinforcement is dependent on a string of Rv's of a certain kind, these
responses may be set up by a text. So, if you are going to take a course or
take a test on Skinner, a text can set up the Rv chains that may be available
later and be reinforced when they occur. As Skinner has said, notebooks
and libraries are not filled with facts and definitions; they contain marks on
pieces of paper which are discriminative stimuli for talking. With a text even
I can talk about physics the way Einstein did. And I don't have to do what
he did to get that verbal behavior; I couldn't. Textuals give us the behavior
of people long dead and far away. They may properly be said to be a way of
storing behavior, rather than information. The point is this. Reading gives
us verbal behavior which someone else may reinforce. You don't get reinforcement for speaking unless you speak, and important sources of strength
for speaking are the discriminative stimuli of a text.

Even if someone else will not reinforce me for verbal responses set up by texts, it is often reinforcing to read. This may be because it is reinforcing just to be able to speak, perhaps in order to prevent the environment from becoming too quiet. Also, this is reinforcing in the same way that going to a play is, or watching TV is. It permits me to talk about experiences that I have never had. Very importantly, it may provide me with behavior that competes with and crowds out other behavior, where this other behavior has aversive properties. It is a means of escaping, not from my unpleasant thoughts, but from my aversive behavior. I talk to myself a great deal, almost all the time, in fact. And some of the things I hear are negative conditioned reinforcers. Reading is a good way of preventing these from occurring. And it also is an easy way of acquiring some positive conditioned reinforcers.

9

intraverbals

DEFINITION AND PARADIGM

AN INTRAVERBAL IS ANY VERBAL OPERANT WHOSE CONTROL-LING VARIABLE IS THE SPEAKER'S OWN PRIOR VERBAL BEHAVIOR. There are several subvarieties of intraverbals, so it is impossible to be more specific about the form of the response term in operants of this sort in this definition. The following illustration shows the paradigm for a simple intraverbal and includes a notation convention that we have used before. $Rv:S^D$ is a

$$Rv: S^D \text{ "TABLE"} \longrightarrow Rv \text{ "CHAIR"}$$

symbol that denotes the case where the stimulus is itself generated by a previous response. This event is usually audible, and always proprioceptive, that is, the previous response has internal stimulus consequences mediated via neural receptors at the joints and muscles.

Let me explain this again. Remember that each time a person talks his muscles move. And, we know that he can respond to the movements themselves as well as to the sounds they produce when he speaks aloud. So these movements as well as the audible sounds become discriminative stimuli.

Here are some examples. They will get you speaking *textually*. When they stop, what you go on to say to yourself is a Rv that is part of an intraverbal—it is under the control of *your* previous Rv's.

100

A stitch in time saves . . .

A penny saved is a penny . . .

Shakespeare was born in . . .

That is, you will speak on if the sounds you make while reading are discriminative stimuli for your intraverbals. The first two discriminative stimuli exert strong and precise control for nearly every person who speaks English. The last controls many different Rv's; some are weak, some are strong but idiosyncratic, such as "bed." And some people don't have any intraverbal Rv's under the control of the last discriminative stimulus. These people often say nothing. The point of these examples is that once we begin speaking, we alter our stimulus circumstances by producing additional discriminative stimuli which evoke other Rv's. These changes in the discriminative stimuli present help keep us talking. This process may go on and on, so that once we start, we often continue speaking with no stimulus control but our own speech. Intraverbally generated discriminative stimuli are ubiquitous and inescapable, and thus they account for a great deal of what gets said. Intraverbals must constitute the biggest class of verbal operants, for almost nothing that is said seems to be completely free of intraverbal controlling relations.

There are two main classes or subdivisions of intraverbals because for each class somewhat different reinforcement contingencies are at work. IN CHAINS, REINFORCEMENT IS CONTINGENT UPON THE OCCURRENCE OF CERTAIN RV'S IN A FIXED ORDER. These tend to be grammatically intact, although sometimes criticized as being merely due to rote memorization, such as the Rv "7 x 9 = 63." CLUSTERS ARE RV'S THAT USUALLY, BUT NOT ALWAYS, CORRESPOND CLOSELY TO LEXICAL WORDS, WHICH TEND TO EVOKE ONE ANOTHER WITHOUT ANY FIXED ORDERING; THEY TEND TO BE AGRAMMATICAL. The word-association studies let us know about a lot of these, for example, "table"—"chair." We will explore the properties and reinforcement histories of each of these subspecies of intraverbals in some detail in the remainder of this chapter.

HOW INTRAVERBALS ARE REINFORCED

What follows here is a somewhat overgeneralized account. Not all intraverbals will be seen to conform to this pattern, but we will go into the special modifications of the main story as we come to the special subvarieties of intraverbals. Basically, intraverbals come about because reinforcement for verbal behavior is usually intermittent and comes after extended speaking. Suppose a man speaks, gets no reinforcer, but continues speaking. If he eventually gets a reinforcer, the following is the situation. Because his utterance was an extended one, in its second part he has spoken in the presence of the sounds and feels of his earlier speaking and has been reinforced. Those sounds and feels of the earlier speaking are stimuli in the presence of which speaking was reinforced. They thus become discriminative stimuli for the Rv's that follow them.

It is also generally true that operants of all sorts, *both verbal and nonverbal*, are usually only reinforced intermittently. The intermittency of reinforcement for operants is itself caused. Intermittent reinforcement for verbal behavior is generally not due to explicit programming on the part of the reinforcement mediator. Rather, because reinforcement mediators seldom perform their roles in an explicitly instructional way, they may be unaware that they reinforce the speaker or fail to do so on any particular occasion. The mediator talks or acts in such ways that bring reinforcement to *him*. That the speaker is also reinforced is often incidental to the mediator. Sometimes both may have to wait a while. The first part of the next illustration shows some S^D's for tacts. If the speaker just tacted

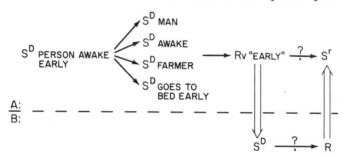

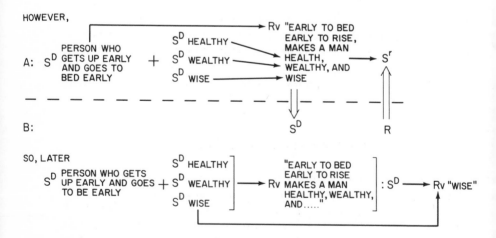

"early," the hearer doesn't get much of a useful discriminative stimulus. In general, fragmentary tacting is useless to the hearer because it does not provide him with sufficient discriminative stimuli for him to behave in such a way as to be reinforced. So, if the speaker, as in the second part of the illustration, tacts in an extended fashion, that behavior is reinforceable (it provides the hearer with an adequate discriminative stimulus) and it is sometimes reinforced. Note that not all of the Rv's were immediately reinforced. A Rv may occur several times in an extended utterance before reinforcement occurs. Thus the reinforcement for operants with that Rv is intermittent.

Now see what happens if we pick *any* Rv in an utterance and characterize its reinforcement history. In this case our Rv is "wise." First, we may notice that everything prior to that Rv can be considered as a stimulus, albeit generated by the speaker himself. The lowest part of the illustration shows this. The Rv's encased by the bracket are discriminative stimuli, auditory ones if the verbal behavior is overt, as it sometimes is, and proprioceptive if the verbal behavior is covert *or* overt. Remember, self-produced small stimuli are legitimate. The speaker can see, feel, and hear his muscle-produced body movements. Thus the next time the speaker Rv:S^D's "early to bed and early to rise, makes a man healthy, wealthy, and . . . ," the Rv "wise" is likely to occur. The subsequent recurrence of the Rv "wise" in the presence of such stimuli, that is, the strength of the intraverbal, depends upon how often "wise" has occurred and been reinforced in that situation. The number of reinforcements, the schedule of reinforcement, the magnitude of the reinforcements, and so forth, will all have their usual effects on these intraverbal operants. These other variables, in turn, will depend in large part upon the nature of the speaker's environment in the past. For most speakers in the United States, the Rv:S^D "early to bed and early to rise" has been very common in the past, and associated with considerable reinforcement; hence, the Rv:S^D "early to bed and early to rise, makes a man" controls strong intraverbals. So also does the Rv:S^D "chair"; "table" is the most likely Rv to follow. The Rv:S^D "Shakespeare" is less likely to control much, and the Rv:S^D "eleemosynary" has extremely weak control over any Rv's for most of us. We will now look in greater detail at the first of the two classes of intraverbals, namely, chains.

CHAINS

Much nonverbal behavior consists of chains. For example, the bar-press or key-peck is actually a relatively fixed series of responses. Because it is fixed, it is convenient to view it as a single unitary thing, an act. But actually completion of the act depends upon some stimuli generated by the behavior itself. Here is how Keller and Schoenfeld analyzed the bar-press in 1950:

Stimulus	Response
Bar-location	Approach
Visual bar	Rising
Tactual bar	Pressing
Apparatus noise	Lowering
Visual pellet	Seizing
Pellet-in-mouth	Chewing

That analysis seems just as good today as it did then. We can look at verbal behavior from the same perspective and in so doing find many examples of verbal chaining. *Counting* consists of verbal chains. We may start off with the Rv:S^D "one." This has intraverbal control over many other Rv's. Such control is weak for Rv's such as "them" or "glasses" or "sugar" but is strong for "two." We then have the Rv:S^D "one, two," which has strong controlling properties for several other Rv's, such as "button my shoe," but also "three." Which leaves us with the Rv:S^D "one, two, three." Now, two highly likely Rv's are "go" and "four." If "four" occurs, we have the Rv:S^D "one, two, three, four," and all the rest—i.e., "five, six, seven, . . . "—come tumbling out.

Adages, idioms, and *cliches* have the same feature—if they get started, they rattle off. But not always. Sometimes the speaker lets the hearer finish for himself, as in (here I get you going textually):

Clean as a . . .

Look before you . . .

He who hesitates . . .

Often sound and order are the only reinforceable things about them. Compare "He who hesitates is lost" and "Look before you leap." However, they are very reinforceable. That may be what is so important about them. They may be utter nonsense, but they are both reinforcing and reinforceable. They are similar to advice, which is a conditioned reinforcer for its recipient and generally leads to a conditioned reinforcer for its giver. These features may have helped an unemployed Austrian house painter nearly gain control of the world.

Filler, verbal junk, and *verbal clutter* are some of the names given to such utterances as "I mean," "listen," "say," "know what I mean," and "like." The hearer reinforces the speaker for saying these things, because in the past Rv's such as these may have preceded the hearer's own reinforcement. They can be used to start off chains easily, and are parasitically maintained by the terminal reinforcement for the later components of the chain.

Words, surprisingly, may sometimes be chains of phones. They occasionally get out of order, which is generally a good sign of chaining. College professors, among other lecturers, are usually good sources of disordered phonemic chains in words.

Formulas, including *symbolic logic, higher mathematics, syllogisms,* and *paradigms,* are verbal chains into which other Rv's may be substituted so that the speaker keeps everything straight (gets reinforced). These are usually memorized by rote. This category would include, I think, the mathematical part of Hull's learning theory, for example, as well as any formalized version of natural science theories. *Arithmetic,* for example, the multiplication table, is pure chaining. Problem solving is not; that is why the problems are harder to do. Success in the latter involves knowing *when* to emit *which* chain and is the product of an entirely different reinforcement history.

History is largely composed of chains acquired on the basis of textual or echoic discriminative stimuli. "Caesar crossed the Rubicon" may have been a tact once, in 49 B.C., but it certainly is not one now. We learn these Rv's as words whose order is important. "Shakespeare was born in" belongs to several chains, if you have a reinforcement history for them, such as the ones that end with "England," "Stratford," or "1564."

Be very careful; chaining is *not the source of grammar.* If it does account for some grammatical order, the proportion due to chains is negligible—the grammaticality of adages, cliches, and the like. We emit more nonchains than chains, so grammaticality cannot be due to chaining. We emit lots of verbal behavior that is unique as a string of utterances or Rv's, but is behavior that is grammatical. It is composed of previously learned Rv's, but we never emitted them in that sequence before. We will have to talk about autoclitics to see how this occurs. But the important point is that chains are not the major source of grammaticality.

Chains seem peculiarly likely to break down. This doesn't mean that there is something wrong with either the speaker or this account, because the production of *defective chains* is lawful and occurs for very good reasons, which we can give entirely within the framework of this approach. THERE ARE TWO PRINCIPAL TYPES OF DEFECTIVE CHAINS—HOMOGENEOUS AND OVERWORKED. We will examine each in turn.

Of course, a chain cannot be completely *homogeneous,* for then there would be no differentiation between its parts. BUT IF SOME Rv:S^D's ARE REPETITIVE, THAT IS, IF THEY RECUR OVER AND OVER AGAIN SO THAT SEVERAL PARTS OF THE CHAIN ARE THE SAME, THEY DO NOT CLEARLY INDICATE WHAT COMES NEXT, AND THEN THE SEQUENCE IS A HOMOGENEOUS CHAIN. For example, *tongue twisters* are nearly or relatively homogeneous chains:

"*P*eter *P*iper *p*icked a *p*eck of *p*ickled *p*eppers"

"*S*he *s*ells *s*ea*s*hells by the *s*ea*s*hore"
"A *b*lue *b*ox of *b*aby *b*iscuits"

HAPLOLOGY REFLECTS THE TENDENCY FOR SOME OF THE REPETITIVE MATE-
RIAL, OR SOMETIMES SOME OF THE NONREPETITIVE PARTS OF HOMOGENEOUS
CHAINS, TO DROP OUT. The process produces a form of *defective chain*. This
happens for good reasons though. In such chains some discriminative
stimuli occur several times, as shown in the next illustration. The Rv's that

$$\text{Rv: } S_1^D \longrightarrow \text{Rv: } S_2^D \longrightarrow \text{Rv: } S_3^D \longrightarrow \text{Rv: } S_4^D \longrightarrow \text{Rv: } S_5^D \longrightarrow \text{Rv: } S_6^D$$

WHERE

$$\text{Rv: } S_1^D \; = \; \text{Rv: } S_3^D \; = \; \text{Rv: } S_5^D$$

follow the repetitive Rv:S^D's, then, are likely to occur when any one of the
repetitive Rv:S^D's occurs. For example, Rv:S$^D_6$ is likely to "jump over"
Rv:S$^D_4$ and Rv:S$^D_5$ and occur right after Rv:S$^D_3$ because Rv:S$^D_3$ and Rv:S$^D_5$
are the same. Because the repetitive Rv:S^D's are not unambiguous, the
speaker's Rv's may come further under the control of the nonrepetitive
Rv:S^D's which may crowd out the repetitive ones. This is reflected in some
etymologies:

Narcissusism $\longrightarrow$ narcissism $\longrightarrow$ narcism
Pacificism $\longrightarrow$ pacifism
Barbara $\longrightarrow$ Barbra

Or else, slurring or elision may occur, or an attempt to differentiate the
repetitious Rv:S^D's via inflection may be made.

Our next illustration shows what happens in the development of a species of verbal time bomb called the *overworked chain*. As the top part of the
illustration shows, at first stimulus control between adjacent Rv:S^D pairs is

$$\text{Rv: } S^D \longrightarrow \text{Rv: } S^D \longrightarrow \text{Rv: } S^D \longrightarrow \text{Rv: } S^D \longrightarrow S^r$$
$$\text{Rv: } S^D \longrightarrow \text{Rv: } S^D \longrightarrow \text{Rv: } S^D \longrightarrow \text{Rv: } S^D \longrightarrow S^r$$

built up, but when such linkages have reached maximum strength, more
remote nonadjacent ones can grow, as shown in the bottom part of the illustration. These controlling relations between nonadjacent Rv:S^D's can grow
in strength through continued reinforcement and become as strong as those
between the adjacent Rv:S^D's. THE EFFECT OF ALL THIS IS THAT IN THE

OVERWORKED CHAIN, for any rv:S^D, each Rv in the chain is about equally likely. The links are strong, but they are not tightly kept in place. The result has traditionally been called a *spoonerism*. It was named after an Oxford clergyman who was especially prone to do it, and who is believed to have been the person who first said:

"We will now sing 'Kinkering Kongs.'"

"It is harder for a rich man to get into heaven than for a camel to pass through the knee of an idol."

"In the time of our queer old Dean Victoria."

Spooner wasn't the only one who said things like that. A member of the U.S. House of Representatives' Committee on the Judiciary said, during the hearings on the impeachment of Richard Nixon: "There are those who would fire the fuels of emotion about the work of this committee." The most famous of all spoonerisms, I believe, was Harry Von Zell's massacre of "Herbert Hoover," where in the course of trying to correct himself, he must have done every possible variation of that chain ("Hoobert Heever," "Heeber Hoovert," . . .). That was because "Herbert Hoover" was at that time both overworked and homogeneous. All of this is *misspeaking*, but it isn't "uncaused" or "accidental" or "Freudian." We will now discuss the second kind of intraverbal, clusters.

CLUSTERS

In CLUSTERS, order and grammar are absent. Typically, an array of Rv:S^D's evoke one another with no particular ordering or grammatical relationship among them. That is, Rv:S^D's just form a cluster, members of whick are related to each other simply by their power to evoke each other.

Word-association experiments usually produce data that show clustering. The next illustration displays two examples of the clusters that may be found in word-association experiments; the first is taken from Goodenough and the second from Palermo and Jenkins.

We must be careful in interpreting these two examples. In clustering, the stimulus is a member of each cluster. There are six clusters shown for the Rv:S^D "ring" and eight for the Rv:S^D blue. *Ring* and *blue* are themselves members of each one of those clusters. This gives us a hint as to the criterion for separating chains from clusters in our analysis. CLUSTERS ARE BIDIRECTIONAL, whereas CHAINS ARE NOT BI-DIRECTIONAL. So, "ring"—"worm" isn't really a cluster; it was an intra-verbal chain which was set off by the Rv:S^D "ring." A Rv:S^D such as

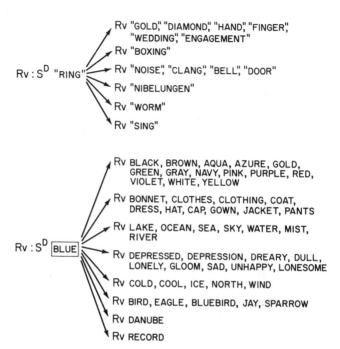

"blue" is a member of several clusters, but notice that other members of any one of these clusters are not members of the others, usually. To tell, see if you can move back and forth along the arrow. "Blue" is a discriminative stimulus for the Rv "lake" and "ocean" is a discriminative stimulus for the Rv "blue," but "ocean" is *not* a discriminative stimulus for the Rv "pink," even though "blue" is.

What all this means, in practical terms, is that a speaker who says "blue" for any reason (and the only reason that *you* would have for saying it now is a textual one) then immediately has available a great deal of verbal behavior; he is able to go on and say something "on his own." He can move along, within and between the clusters controlled by the Rv:S^D "blue." One topic *reminds* him of another, or he makes *allusions*, and so forth. These often reflect the effects of two kinds of clusters: formal clusters and thematic clusters.

INTRAVERBAL THEMATIC CLUSTERS ARE DEFINED NEGATIVELY, THAT IS, BY EXCLUSION. THERE IS NO ACOUSTIC SIMILARITY BETWEEN THE Rv:S^D AND THE Rv THAT IT CONTROLS. This leads to the name *thematic*. Even though they don't sound alike, two Rv's in any one thematic cluster are "about the same thing," for example, lake, ocean, sky. They still aren't chains, because the bidirectionality criterion is met. So, in the preceding illustration all the remaining intraverbals controlled by the Rv:S^D "ring" are thematic clusters *except* for the intraverbal Rv:S^D→Rv "sing."

Psychologists have collected a huge amount of data on intraverbal thematic clusters. The word-association studies started with those of Galton and continue to the present day. This is where most of the experimental data on verbal behavior come from. All the collections of word norms from those of Kent and Rosanoff to those of today (e.g., Palermo and Jenkins) show the existence of intraverbals and their commonality among speakers. Here are some examples. I will not describe these experiments from which they come in detail, nor will I cite them with full academic rigor; they are merely illustrative.

Bousfield had subjects read mixed lists that contained animal names, proper names, names of professions, and names of vegetables, all scrambled in a random arrangement. When asked to recall the words on the list, the subjects' Rv's appeared in thematic clusters.

Jenkins and Russell read aloud to subjects disarranged stimulus-response pairs from the earlier Kent and Rosanoff study. Subjects were later asked to recall the words that they had heard. If a subject recalled a word, he usually recalled its associate immediately afterward.

Howes and Osgood explored the method of *saturating stimuli.* They gave their subjects stimuli composed of a string of four words and told them to associate to the last word. For example, some subjects received the stimulus "429, 124, 713, dark," while others received "devil, eat, basic, dark," and still others heard "devil, fearful, sinister, dark." By putting more of a cluster into the stimulus, the probability of a Rv from the rest of the cluster rose. So that in the previous examples the Pr (Rv "hell") was greater for each of the stimuli as the number of "neutral" stimulus words declined.

Howes and Osgood also investigated the *proximity effect.* This may best be defined by an example. The discriminative stimulus "bull" belongs to several clusters, each of which has other members, such as sex—"cow," age—"calf," clumsy— "in a china closet." So if the discriminative stimulus is "feminine, clumsy, young, bull" and the subject is instructed to respond to the last word, the Rv "calf" is likely. But if "young" is moved away from "bull" in the stimulus, the Pr (Rv "calf") goes down.

Judson and Cofer examined what may be called the *prior entry effect.* Subjects were presented multiword stimuli, such as "skyscraper, temple, cathedral, prayer," and were instructed to indicate whichever one didn't belong. Now, "cathedral" and "temple" each belong to at least two thematic groups—religion and edifices. So, most subjects will indicate that "prayer" does not belong, because the initial "skyscraper" taps the edifice cluster. However, if subjects are devout churchgoers, "skyscraper" will be chosen as not belonging. This is understandable, for such subjects more reinforcements have occurred for Rv's in the religious cluster.

Foley and Macmillan looked at the *special reinforcement history ef-*

fect. They looked at the different associations of law school, medical school, and psychology students to such words as "administer," "complaint," "cell" ("sell"). As you might imagine, given the S^D "administer," the medical students came up with Rv's such as "aid," "dose," "drug," "first aid," "medicine," "syringe," and "treat"; while the law students gave "estate," "govern," "judge," "law," "money," and "oath." Different reinforcement histories (backgrounds) had differentially strengthened different clusters in the two groups.

Literally hundreds of word-association studies have been reported. There were so many studies that H. C. Warren, whose *History of the Association Psychology* was published in 1921, could not even list them all. He pointed out that in the classical word-association literature, certain rational classificatory schemes had been proposed. For example, apple-red was said to show defining; rose-flower, superordination; flower-rose, subordination; man-woman, common accompaniment; and dark-light, opposites. But Warren was forced to conclude, as we know that he must, that this sort of hierarchical classificatory enterprise led nowhere. There is no functional or dynamic difference among these cluster pairs. Their fit, or lack of fit, into various classificatory schemes doesn't tell us anything useful.

Once we know about thematic clusters, we are in a position to explain the phenomenon that has variously been termed *mediated generalization* or *semantic generalization*. The next illustration, which shows this phenomenon paradigmatically, is taken from Mednick. Part I of the illustration represents the presenting of the word *light* written on a piece of paper and an electric shock to a fluent speaker of English. In Part II we see represented the result of presenting the word *dark*, which had never been paired with the shock. Mediated generalization was supposed to be a terrible problem for stimulus-response psychology and a great embarrassment to it. Remember that SIMPLE STIMULUS GENERALIZATION IS THE TENDENCY FOR STIMULI OTHER THAN THE ONE INVOLVED IN ORIGINAL CONDITIONING TO EVOKE THE SAME RESPONSE. The common cases occur when the two (or more) stimuli fall along the same physical dimension, or have common elements or accompany each other as part of clusters. Well, clearly, if we have an English-speaking subject, and he does what is diagrammed in Parts I and II of the illustration, it is generalization. But it certainly isn't simple stimulus generalization, and it wouldn't work with a pigeon or a speaker of French. Also, don't be deceived here; I am not trying to sneak in a blurring of the operant versus respondent distinction. The GSR (galvanic skin response) is a respondent phenomenon, a change in the electrical resistance of the skin. But if we take everything into account, as shown in Parts I and II' of the illustration, then we see that this effect turns out to be a convenient indicator that something else, operant behavior, is going on. So, al-

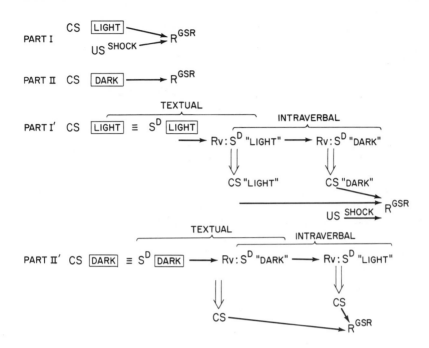

though the measured effect is itself not verbal, its occurrence depends upon a special verbal conditioning history.

What does the mediating are the Rv:S^D's in the braces. These are conditioned covert operants, whose stimulus properties serve as CS's for the respondents. So we see, in Part I' of the illustration, that what appeared to be just a CS is also a discriminative stimulus for a textual, that is, the speaker is disposed to say "light." By virtue of the past history of reinforcement which has made him a fluent speaker of English, when he is disposed to say "light", he is also likely to say the Rv's with which "light" clusters—"dark," "heavy," and so forth. So these Rv's, such as "dark," occur before the shock and get the GSR conditioned to their proprioceptive stimulus consequences. Then when dark is presented on the paper, a textual occurs and also sets off an intraverbal, both of which help to elicit the GSR, as shown in Part II' of the illustration. Finally, we can state a LAW FOR MEDIATED GENERALIZATION: IF A NEW RESPONSE IS CONDITIONED TO ONE MEMBER OF A THEMATIC CLUSTER, IT MAY BE EVOKED BY THE OTHER MEMBERS OF THAT CLUSTER.

IN AN INTRAVERBAL FORMAL CLUSTER THE CONTROLLED AND CONTROLLING Rv'S SOUND LIKE EACH OTHER. BUT THE ACOUSTIC SIMILARITY IS ONLY PARTIAL. THE RESPONSES DO NOT ACOUSTICALLY REPRODUCE THE STIMULUS, AS IN THE TRUE ECHOIC. Also, here the discriminative stimulus is self-generated.

Kent and Rosanoff called responses of this sort "clangs" when they occurred in word-association experiments. For example, if the Rv:S^D is "ring," the following formal cluster members occur: "sing," "bing," "ting," "ping," "ming," "wing," "zing," "spring," "sling," and so forth. Formal clustering is not restricted to the word-association experiment. Rhyming poetry is verbal behavior where some responses of formal clusters appear in certain specified places.

An implication of the definition of formal clusters is that if a sound occurs in one's own speech, it tends to recur soon. Such sounds tend to cluster. Skinner reported his investigation of this in his paper "A Quantitative Estimate of Certain Types of Sound-Patterning in Poetry." Putting this another way, the intervals between the same phonemes, words, or phrases are not randomly distributed. They are too short. Here is a heuristic example: If there were twenty /p/'s in a four-hundred-phoneme sample, then the mean number of phonemes between /p/'s would be twenty, and the distribution

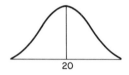 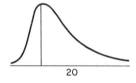

NUMBER OF PHONEMES BETWEEN EACH /p/

of the number of other phonemes between successive occurrences of /p/ would look like that shown on the left side of the above illustration, if it were governed by a random process. But, if in fact the process were not random, the actual distribution would look like that pictured on the right side of the illustration. That is, the number of other phonemes occurring between successive occurrences of /p/ would be much smaller, and these small gaps between /p/'s would occur more often than would be expected by chance. The /p/'s would bunch up. Well, the real result of this clustering is that casual, "spontaneous," nonliterary, nonoratorical speech is alliterative, rhyming, assonant. The interesting case is that of phonemic or phonetic clustering. Sometimes the results are rather painful. The following quotation originally appeared in a serious book review by McNeil: "Since the intentions of the authors are more modest than the dust-jacket's encomium, they should be spared the odium of being the heralds of psychology's millennium." A professor of psychology was overheard saying: "I have no rapport with Rappoport, but he is wrapped up in it . . ."

Skinner studied formal clustering experimentally. He invented a device that he called the *verbal summator*, which is a kind of verbal projective test. It consisted of a phonograph record composed only of vowel sounds: *a, e, i, ah, oh, oo.* These were arranged in intervals of 3, 4, 5, with two always accented, for example, *ah´ oh oh oo´*. The subject in the experiment listens to the record until he can "hear what it is saying," although, in fact, nothing is being said. The following is a sample protocol, which Skinner collected and reported in *Verbal Behavior*:

"elle n'est partie"
"do not say your part"
"take leave of it"
"oh, are you"
"got your visa"
"elle ne sait pas"
"p-p-partie"
"are you going"
"who are you"
"vis-à-vis"

Sherlock Holmes would say: "Elementary, my dear Watson; the subject speaks French and is about to go on a journey." However, we see that much of the subject's verbal behavior is simply echoic, but not self-echoic. The vowels of the responses tend to echo—i.e., match—those of the sample sequence on the record; their number and stress match too.

But importantly for our purposes here, the verbal summator has no consonants. Remember that intraverbals can occur between parts of words. So all consonants in the subject's responses are intraverbally controlled. The stimuli that evoke the consonants are the vowel sounds of the record which the speaker echoes, and the consonants that he has just emitted before as part of "telling what is on the record." They occur entirely too often to have been lifted from the record or standard English. Also, the following Rv's occur two or three times: "part," "visa," "ait-pas." These facts show the extreme constriction of Rv forms; just a few things get said, one or two small formal clusters, and that is about it.

Thematic clustering shows up too. We can see it in this protocol; lacking anything on the stimulus side to narrow it thematically, it narrowed itself. It all seems to be about a trip to France. This is because the Rv's are weakly controlled by the discriminative stimuli from the record. So, although it doesn't always happen, here at least we got formal clustering within a thematic cluster.

Bruce found a similar thematic clustering effect in a different experiment. He played recorded lists of words with a background of white noise. He found that his subjects misidentified the words on the record but put the errors in the same thematic groups as the words they correctly recognized. That is, parts of the body or foods were identified as separate clusters, and each cluster included words that the subjects said they heard but which weren't on the record. Extracluster errors were rare.

Explicit reproduction of rhyme and alliteration requires, in the first place, that the speaker have an intraverbal formal repertoire. Skinner has shown that Shakespeare, in his sonnets, didn't alliterate any more than might have been expected on the basis of normal speech. He "might well have drawn his words out of a hat." Swinburne, on the other hand, was, according to Skinner's research, very much an alliterator.

There is an explanation for formal clustering. It is a form of response induction. This process has been frequently observed in nonverbal behavior. RESPONSE INDUCTION IS THE TENDENCY OF RESPONSES SIMILAR IN FORM TO THE ONE THAT WAS REINFORCED TO OCCUR IN THE SAME SITUATION IN WHICH REINFORCEMENT WAS DELIVERED. Response induction is caused by the genetic constitution of mammals. It occurs in bar-pressing, key-pecking, and also talking. So, if a rat was reinforced for pressing a bar with a force of 21 grams, he is likely to press it with a force of 20 or 22 or 29 or 23 grams. Similarly, if a man is reinforced for saying "ring," he is likely to say "sing."

10

multiple causation

"And that," said Jack, "is that." We have run through all the primary variables that control verbal behavior. We looked at each one as if it existed by itself in a one-variable universe and acted all alone. We try to arrange situations of that sort in the laboratory, where our control of other variables lets exactly one variable work at any one time. The world of the laboratory is just as "real" as the world outside it; the world inside the laboratory is not fictional. But in the extralaboratory world, many variables are present at any one time and they interact. Like nonverbal behavior, verbal behavior is multicontrolled. Our previous chapters have considered each antecedent controller of behavior as the sole operative variable. This was for ease of definition and exposition. Now we have to put the variables together and show how they interact to produce observable nonlaboratory verbal behavior.

PROBLEMS ARISING FROM MULTIPLE CAUSATION

A given speech interval contains responses contributed by several different controlling variables. I'll present some examples, which are far from all the possibilities; working out all the combinations would merely be busywork.

Multiple tacts: "My new white silk shirt"

Mand + Audience: "John, look . . . "

Tact + Echoic: "You said 'hello.'"

Textual + Intraverbal: Your verbal behavior after you read "Early to bed and early to rise, makes a man . . ."

Reading aloud, which is mostly pure textuals, can have "mistakes." These are usually due to the intrusion of intraverbals which are stronger than the textuals, so these mistakes are Textuals + Intraverbals.

These examples are not merely an exercise. They support the point that at one level of analysis each component of speech is "nothing but" conditioned operants. Thus it is like key-pecks and bar-presses. At this level, verbal operants are nothing new, and nothing that was never previously reinforced ever happens. That is supposed to be the big defect of the whole approach. It seems to make no provision for creative verbal behavior, for spontaneous speech. However—and this is the important *however* that some people seem to have skipped—the utterance as a whole may be insightful, creative, new, never said before by either the speaker or anyone else. Even though whole utterances may have never previously occurred and been reinforced, their components have. The next illustration gives a simple example. If I can tact the moon and green cheese, as in the

$$S^D \text{ MOON} \longrightarrow \text{Rv "THE MOON"}$$
$$S^D \text{ COLOR} \longrightarrow \text{Rv "GREEN CHEESE"}$$
$$\text{SO}$$
$$\begin{array}{c} S^D \text{ MOON} \\ + \\ S^D \text{ COLOR} \end{array} \longrightarrow \text{Rv "THE MOON....GREEN CHEESE"}$$

upper part of the illustration, then when the two discriminative stimuli occur together, I can tact them both, as shown in the lower part of the figure. Remember, if at some time, somewhere else, a variable acquires control of a response, if the variable occurs again, even if in a new combination with other variables, the response is likely to occur too. It drops into all sorts of behavior, "all at once."

So, if the discriminative stimulus *yellow-green book* is presented to a speaker, and his Rv "chartreuse" is reinforced in its presence, whenever anything yellow-green next occurs in the speaker's environment, he is likely to say "chartreuse," as in "chartreuse liqueur" or "the dress is chartreuse." These examples are similar to the case of the man who learned to say "moon" to one discriminative stimulus and "green cheese" to another, and then said "the moon is green cheese" when the two discriminative stimuli occurred at the same time. Let's look at another more complex example of this process. If a child who is learning to talk learns one intraverbal such as "ex" as part of "express," it *appears all at once* in every other word that he either already knows or will learn. Thus it may replace "es," say, in "explain," "explore," "extra," and so forth. Previously, he might have said "esplain" or "esplore" or "estra." The discriminative stimulus that came to control the Rv "ex" in the context of "express" was present all along when "es" was previously said in "esplain," "espress," and so forth. So when the Rv "ex" got conditioned to that discriminative stimulus it crowded out "es" and was said whenever the discriminative stimulus occurred and produced the child's knowing how to say "explore" and "extra" without any obvious history of reinforcement for pronouncing these words correctly.

Furthermore, any one variable controls more than one Rv. The next illustration shows how this applies to all the primary variables and their corresponding operant classes that we have examined.

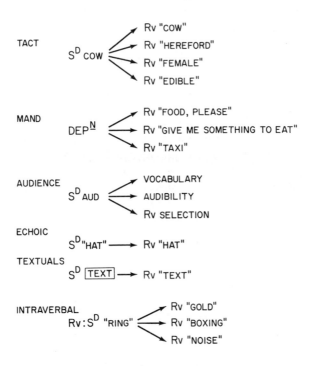

At first, this seems to be all to our benefit. Because people talk so much, it is reassuring to see that an apparently constant environment can control (generate) a great deal of verbal behavior. We don't need a barrage or progression of constantly varying controlling variables; a "static" environment is potent enough. Furthermore, as systematic theorists we can look good. We can usually give a plausible reconstruction of any actual Rv. If we know what is said, we can be confident that we can find some controlling variable or relation present.

But in the long run we have an embarrassment of riches. We have given the speaker too much to say. We must explain what determines which Rv occurs, because not all of those that are likely at any one time do appear. Some process smoothly and quickly determines which will get said.

Traditionally it was said that the speaker "chooses his words," but there is hardly time for *that*. An accomplished speaker doesn't stop to choose before each word or sentence. Furthermore, that theory reflects a bad scientific logic. If there is a chooser, he must be located and his choosing behavior must be accounted for. So, actually *choosing* is not a solution. It is merely pushing the problem backward into some unknown or unknowable domain.

Suppose we are able to find out what variable is operative at the time the speaker speaks. We then have to predict what he will say. Another tradition, that of stimulus-response psychology, advised predicting the strongest operant, namely, the operant that had the most favorable (in terms of the schedule and number of reinforcers and their magnitude) reinforcement history. If an operant has had the most favorable reinforcement history, its Rv should be the most probable Rv. This solution works sometimes; if you stick to it, you will be right more often than not in the long run. But, weak or rare Rv's do occur, and their appearance has to be explained. Hull's solution made this a spontaneous process, which is not very good science either. After carefully pinning response probability down to several decimal places, he put in a random oscillatory variable. Where it was in the world, no one knew. But, it produced strange results, according to the theory. Response probability would swoop up and down apparently on its own! Therefore, according to this theory, a rare response occurs when its oscillatory inhibition is momentarily low and the oscillatory inhibition of all the others is momentarily high.

We can do better and stay within the confines of the natural science limitations that we have imposed upon ourselves. Help is at hand, because any response, including Rv's, may be controlled by more than one variable. Another way of saying this is: All Rv's are members of more than one verbal operant.

Here is another example which makes the point. Consider a man who says "oil." On some occasions it may be a mand, as in "Oil that door; it squeaks." On other occasions it may be a tact, as when the man from the drilling rig ran to the ranch house yelling "Oil, oil." It may be to a great degree under audience control. This is the hardest to see. But if you were introduced to an audience composed of Mr. Getty, Mr. Rockefeller, the king of Saudi Arabia, and the sheik of Kuwait, sooner or later you would be likely to say "oil." That "oil" is part of textuals or echoics is obvious. And finally here is an intraverbal example (read it aloud and listen to yourself): "The sultan of Turkey has a terrible temper. If you make a mistake, he will boil you in . . . ''

How all this helps us out with the prediction problem can be seen if we first recall what we know about supplementary strengthening. The first two parts of the next illustration show this paradigmatically. If the same Rv is put under the control of two separate variables on two separate occasions,

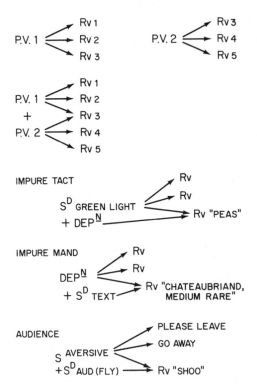

then it may occur once when the two primary variables are concurrently active. That is, if two controlling variables for the same Rv are present at the same time, the effect on Rv probability is additive. So, one response from among the many that might be said, given one variable, may get supplementary strengthening from some other variable. Thus an otherwise very weak response to only one controlling variable may occur because it gets supplementary sources of strength from other concurrently present primary variables. If so, the problems of response competition, occurrence of rare Rv's, and prediction of what the speaker will say are automatically resolved. The rest of the illustration gives some examples of this. Oddly, we knew it all along. Another old example is that we noticed a tendency for echoics and textuals to show up in conversations about something else; prominent signs or words intrude and "remind us of something else."

Following is a new example of supplementary strengthening, which I will go through in some detail. It is extremely common because we cannot escape the concurrent action of primary controlling variables. It is called *thematic overlap*.

Recall that the Rv:S^D "ring" is a member of several clusters, one of which contains the Rv "boxing" and another of which contains the Rv "engagement." Since "ring" is a Rv that is common to these two clusters, they overlap. Now, the following actually happened. As you probably know, Joe Louis wound up owing the U.S. government a lot of money in unpaid income taxes. So, when he finished his career as a boxer, he had to go to work, and he found that he was offered a number of positions as a referee for fights. At his first public appearance in this new role, a television announcer said: "This is the first refereeing engagement he has accepted since he retired from _____." The last Rv could have been "fighting," "boxing," or "competition." But it wasn't; it was "the ring," "fighting," "boxing," and "competition" were likely responses, but "the ring" was even more likely; it was strong for two reasons, both thematic. "Boxing," "fighting," and "competition" don't have good thematic cluster connections with "engagement," but "ring" does.

This example may not be impressive by itself, but I'll give you some more to support the following PRINCIPLE OF THEMATIC OVERLAP. IF A RESPONSE IS A MEMBER OF TWO OR MORE THEMATIC CLUSTERS, SEVERAL OF WHICH ARE CONCURRENTLY STRONG, THE EFFECT ON Rv PROBABILITY IS ADDITIVE. The illustrations are easy to find.

1. "If specificity is a live issue, it is going to haunt us."
2. "Mother sat up all night listening to the radio, which gave a blow-by-blow description of the hurricane."
3. "When I was a graduate student there was a tremendous trend along this line to do trend tests."
4. "I hear that you are going to have surgery. I hope everything comes out all right."
5. "The plumber is too noisy. I can't think; tell him to pipe down."
6. "Experiments in raising chimpanzees in the dark have been very illuminating."
7. "Despite all the work on electrical stimulation of the brain, we have made little headway in understanding all the mechanisms involved."

You try one. "We decided against going out for more beer because a storm was _____ " It (thematic overlap) is said to be the basis of humor. I don't know why it is funny. And it happens easily, even in tragic circumstances; so it isn't intentional. According to Skinner, Amelia Earhart Putnam's husband said of the flight on which she disappeared: "This was to have been her last grave undertaking."

Ambiguity as such isn't humorous. But it may be the basis of style. Shakespeare had so much thematic overlap in *Hamlet* that no one has ever been sure what the play "really" was about at the thematic level. That's why we have all those different interpretations. He did it in the other plays too. They are all great literature, but never funny, especially the "comedies." James Joyce did both thematic and formal overlap deliberately. He supposedly went to the trouble of keeping lists of words to incorporate into his works. As the books of Hayman and Higginson show, the "Anna Livia Plurabelle" section of *Finnegans Wake* is a prime example of a conscious exercise in thematic formal overlap.

STRICTLY SPEAKING, FORMAL OVERLAP OCCURS WHEN ONE MEMBER OF A THEMATIC CLUSTER (WHICH IS STRONG FOR SOME OTHER REASON) GET SUPPLEMENTARY STRENGTH FROM ANOTHER PRIOR RESPONSE THAT IS FORMALLY SIMILAR TO IT.

Poetry, of course, is one of the best sources of examples. Here one emits the Rv that is thematically strong *and* formally similar to a certain preceding Rv (the word with which it rhymes).

Cliches show formal overlap:

"Good as gold"
"Bold as brass"
"Fit as a fiddle"

They are just cliches, even though they have widespread appeal. Isn't it interesting to see the "great truths" of human wisdom resting solidly on a basis of formal overlap? Moreover, if two members of a single thematic cluster also are formally similar, the effect is overwhelming. If one gets said, it almost guarantees that the other will be:

"Spic and span"
"Hem and haw"
"Wrack and ruin"
"Bag and baggage"
"Hale and hearty"
"Vim and vigor"

MISSPEAKING

If you listen carefully to what someone says, especially by listening to a tape recording of his speaking, you may hear the result of a supplementary variable that contributed a Rv it controlled, even when it wasn't needed. Sometimes response competition is a problem; failures to resolve it quickly often lead to misspeaking. This is to be expected. If supplementary variables contribute to response probability, they should reveal themselves clearly, for they are not weak controllers. So, supplementary variables can often be seen to strengthen verbal behavior that is recognized as being "wrong" if it is noticed at all. These occurrences are lawful, as Freud was the first to point out. But, I claim that his explanation of why they occurred was the thing that was wrong. The following classes of examples are probably not homogeneous on either the cause or the effect side, but that's what you'd expect with multiple causation.

INTRUSIONS OCCUR WHEN A Rv THAT IS LIKELY BECAUSE OF A SUPPLEMENTARY VARIABLE'S PRESENCE DISPLACES A WEAKER ONE. A congressman at the Nixon impeachment hearings said: "Few, any, none, of the things done by the special unit were national security." Another said: "Too many members are beginning to think that they are casting the final decision here." And a woman redecorating her house said: "We can put a walker, I mean, a little runner, in the hall."

DISTORTIONS OCCUR WHEN A THEMATICALLY STRONG Rv DISPLACES A FORMALLY SIMILAR ONE. The decorating woman was also a critic of medical practice and said: "You do not subscribe a drug just because you don't know why someone is having a seizure." In her redecorating she got a new stove, for "the old stove blew up because the pilot light was jimmy-rigged." And some of the congressmen found the testimony hard to believe; one said: "It seems to me rather incredulous . . . "

BLENDS MAKE US SUSPECT ABOUT EQUAL STRENGTHENING AND IMPERFECT RESOLUTION OF RESPONSE COMPETITION. Lewis Carroll was a master blender and was responsible for "fuming" + "furious"—"fumious"; "bright" + "glittering"—"brillig"; and "merry" + "whimsey"—"mimsey." A radio commentator explained some of the activities at the impeachment hearings as follows: "Now she is talking about the transformation from the Kennedy administration to the Johnson administration" (transition + transfer). A woman was offered a policewoman's purse and said: "If I buy that purse, I'll look like an underclothes woman" (undercover agent + plainclothes woman). This isn't limited to portmanteau words—it also occurs as phrase blends, such as "hemming and hawing about the bush," "for that matter of fact," "it is easier for a rich man to pass through a camel than get into heaven," "when the gum will grow back, I have no way of saying," "I am so muddle brained."

FOLK ETYMOLOGIES ARE DISTORTIONS OF EXOTIC OR DIFFICULT WORDS WHICH USUALLY SHOW A SUPPLEMENTARY INFLUENCE. THEY ARE USUALLY COMBINATIONS OF PARTIAL ECHOICS, PLUS FORMAL OR THEMATIC FRAGMENTS IN A BLEND. Palmer compiled an entire dictionary of them and was able to indicate some of their sources. Here are some of them:

alabaster—yellow plaster

awnderne—hand iron

apoplexy—happy plex

"the ship sailed round the antipathies (antipodes)"

"the aquarium (requiem) service for the deceased pope"

"my husband is a regular siphon (cipher)"

"he tells antidotes (anecdotes) of his youth"

"her child died, and she went into asterisks (hysterics)"

"they had the bands (banns) put up"

blue as azure—blue as a razor

Court of Common Pleas—common place

coquilles Saint Jacques—Jack's cookies

contra danse—country dance

duplex—double x

fledermaus—flinty mouse

threshold—fresh wood

a widow by grace (an unwed mother)—grace widow—grass widow (a woman whose husband is gone to the golf course most of the time)

gar—gar fish—guard fish

emigrate—hammergrate

harpoon—harping iron

hysterics—high strikes

halter—holder

homily—humble

iota—hooter—hoot (so the folks now say: "I don't give a hoot")

jaundice—janders

jasmin—Jessie's flower

gendarmes—Johnny darbies

jay bird—joy bird

canker—kangaroo

quelque chose (French for "something")—kick shoes

lectern—lant horn

Lenten lilies—lanthorn lilies

lilac—lily oak

mermaid—merry maid

nonchalance—nine shillings

acorn—oak corn

panther—painter

penthouse—paint house

peony rose—piano rose

plaice (a kind of fish)—plash fluke

pomegranate—pound garnet

cushion—question

lamprey—ramper eel

reindeer—ranged deer

reynard (French for "fox")—Reynolds

celery—salary

sexton—saxon

scion—science

c'est autre chose (French for "it's something else")— another pair of
    shoes

scurrility—squirrility

St. Vitus dance—St. Viper's dance

gossamer—summer goose

telegraph—talley graft

delerium tremens—triangles

thwarts—thoughts

toilette—twilight

watercress—water grass

            —water crashes

            —water creases

Even Shakespeare did this: "The best courtier of them all could never have
brought her to such a canary" (quandary) in *Merry Wives of Windsor*;
"civil as an orange" (Seville) in *Much Ado About Nothing*.

Finally, if words are fairly strongly related intraverbally, they sound
well together (are reinforceable) even if they are complete nonsense, as in
"Troops are being flown into Vietnam by the truckload." Or as the movie
actress said, "I made twice as much money as Calvin Coolidge put together."

VERBAL ENGINEERING

Sometimes verbal behavior must be delivered according to some prior specification. This presents a problem for us in our role as engineers, for we have no direct access to, and cannot directly manipulate, speech itself. We solve this problem in a way that reveals a very important principle, one that underlies the whole Skinnerian approach. We manipulate the variables of which the desired behavior is a function. There are two general subclasses of manipulation—the prompt and the probe.

PROMPTS OCCUR WHEN THE FORM OF THE DESIRED VERBAL BEHAVIOR IS SPECIFIED IN ADVANCE. IN PROMPTING, THE ENGINEER SUPPLIES CONTROLLING VARIABLES AND ADDS MORE AND MORE OF THEM UNTIL THE DESIRED SPEECH OCCURS. If I want you to say "Franklin," I may prompt you by supplying you with discriminative stimuli that I believe control that Rv. I do this on the basis of my knowledge or estimate of your past history of reinforcement for speaking. For example, I might say to you:

> "Thomas Jefferson said of him: 'I succeed him; no one could replace him.'"
>
> "He signed both the Declaration of Independence and the U.S. Constitution."
>
> "He opened the Post Office."
>
> "He invented a stove."
>
> "Who invented the rocking chair?"
>
> "Who invented the lightning rod?"
>
> "Who wrote *Poor Richard's Almanac*?"
>
> "He flew a kite in a thunderstorm."
>
> "It begins with an *F*."

PROBES OCCUR WHEN THE CAUSAL VARIABLE IS SPECIFIED IN ADVANCE, AND THE QUESTION IS WHAT VERBAL BEHAVIOR IS CONTROLLED BY IT. Here the subject's repertoire is to be explored, rather than extended. Again, this is usually accomplished by presenting discriminative stimuli of various sorts, as in "What is the difference between formal and thematic clustering?" and "What do you think about abolishing the death penalty for kidnapping?"

All of that is fine, obvious, and agreed to be true by most people just as long as the speaker is someone other than themselves. But—and here is the radical statement—the procedures seem to be the same when we must engineer our own verbal behavior. Even an accomplished speaker does not manipulate his own verbal behavior directly. He can only manipulate the variables of which speech is a function. In other words, the speaker is merely and only a place where variables act, and not a variable himself. He as an entity contributes nothing. Horrors! First Galileo took the earth from the center of the cosmological stage. Then Darwin put man among the animals. Now Skinner is completing Descartes's program and is putting man among the machines. It seems, however, to be a necessary consequence of a strict adherence to scientific materialism.

Let's briefly look at a few examples illustrating self-prompts and self-probes. If you must give a speech, or write a term paper, or play a part, or take a test, you don't just pick out all the relevant words from your vocabulary even though they are all there. You do, however, prompt yourself, usually with textuals, or occasionally with echoics that contain this behavior, that is, you consult books or experts. In acting, one uses intraverbals that are started off by echoics from the person called the prompter.

Traditionally we claim that we "choose our words to express our views or feelings" about capital punishment, or "display our knowledge" about formal and thematic clustering. But what we actually do is inspect our verbal behavior itself, in order to "know our feelings." When presented with a discriminative stimulus such as "What do you think about capital punishment," we probe ourselves. We may start talking aloud, as in dictating a rough draft, or else we may do it covertly. That is, in order to find out what we have to say, we may first listen to what we have to say to ourselves when we talk covertly to ourselves before we speak aloud. We may be able to do this to some extent while speaking aloud, especially if the overt speech is slow and has pauses. We listen to what we have to say about capital punishment, or any other subject matter. One woman was amazingly accurate, but somewhat ingenuous, when she said, "I don't know what I think until I start talking; that's how I find out. I just open my mouth and throw myself into it."

11

autoclitics

The topic of this chapter, autoclitics, is the most subtle part of the theory. It isn't complicated, or hard to understand the way mathematics is, but the processes described here are very busy. It is difficult to see all of their implications at once. Moreover, it is here especially that Skinner's theory runs counter to our traditional views. This is the part of the analysis that has seemed most objectionable to the traditional analysts of speaking and to the new mentalists.

An implication of the aim of the analysis that we have been examining in this book is that all the variables that are necessary and sufficient for generating speaking will be discussed and their effective controlling relationships described. So, we should inquire whether the variables that we have considered and their respective operant classes are sufficient to account for all of speech. In other words, has any known variable been left out, or are there any parts of speech not accounted for? It seems that in all extended utterances except textuals, echoics, and intraverbal chains, there are two response characteristics whose controlling variables have been omitted. Consider the following examples, which I'll go into in detail:

"That man is fat."
"That girl is not fat."
"Everyone is here except John."

"All swans are white."

"Hopefully, the plane will be on time."

Upon looking at these examples, we see our first problem. It appears that some Rv's are not accounted for by the operant classes that we have discussed. Tacts would account for "that man" and "fat," but not "is." We have to find out what controls the Rv "is." It isn't part of a tact for existence; everything exists, so *isness* is wholly nondiscriminable; you can't reinforce in the presence of existence *per se* and extinguish in its absence. In the next utterance—"That girl is not fat"—a tact may account for "that girl," and "fat," in this utterance, may possibly be under echoic or intraverbal control. But, what controls the Rv "is not"? It can't be *absence* in and of itself that controls "is not." For whether she is or is not fat, she always is not a fire engine. Then there is the problem of what controls the "except" in "Everyone is here except John." If "All swans are white," whiteness can be the discriminative stimulus for "white," but all swans cannot be the discriminative stimulus for "all swans." The "hopefully" is supposed to be an adverb modifying "on time." Well, it may be, but that is no scientific explanation of how it got said. In all of our examples of problems we must determine what the controlling variables for these Rv's are, and what their physical loci and compositions are. After all, such Rv's as "is," "is not," "all," and "except" are parts of operants; have been conditioned; and must have causal antecedents. Therefore, part of the job remaining to be finished in this chapter is to identify the causal antecedents for these Rv's and give a plausible account of their conditioning histories.

Controlling variables rarely occur in any special order, again except for those variables that control echoics, textuals, and intraverbal chains. Often controlling variables are concurrent, and if they occur *ad seriatum*, their order does not parallel that of the Rv's. Thus, our second major problem is to account for the ordering of Rv's in speech. For example, the variables that control the Rv "that man" and the Rv "fat" and the Rv "is" occur all at once, but the Rv's do not.

These sorts of words and the ordering of Rv's are said to be "grammatical." So, we have a property of Rv's that may be called grammar. But we do not introduce a grammatical variable. Here grammar is the name of an effect, and not a cause.

DEFINITION AND PARADIGM

Grammatical words and the ordering of Rv's are what Skinner has called *autoclitic* behaviors. I'll give the definition shortly, but first let's ease into it by looking at a paradigm. Autoclitic behavior is a result of a two-stage process, which is shown paradigmatically in the following illustration. In the upper part of the illustration the first stage of the process is

$$S_1^D, S_2^D, \ldots$$
$$DEP_1^N, DEP_2^N, \ldots \left.\right\} \begin{array}{l} \nearrow Rv \\ \leftarrow Rv \\ \leftarrow Rv \\ \searrow Rv \end{array}$$

$$\underbrace{\begin{array}{l} S^{D's} \ OR \\ DEP^{N's} \end{array}}_{} \longrightarrow Rv$$

$$\Downarrow$$

$$S^D \longrightarrow Rv$$

represented. HERE PRIMARY CONTROLLING VARIABLES (P.V.'S), OF THE SORTS THAT WE HAVE DISCUSSED, ARE PRESENT AND ACTIVE AND INCREASE THE CURRENT MOMENTARY PROBABILITY OF THE Rv'S OF SEVERAL OPERANTS. THIS IS CALLED PRIMARY VERBAL BEHAVIOR. STRICTLY SPEAKING, IT IS A COLLECTION OF PRIMARY OPERANTS. These operants may be mands, tacts, intraverbal clusters, small chains, echoics, audience-controlled Rv's, or anything we have examined so far, all jumbled up in no particular order. The speaker now has the ability to speak—"he has something to say." For example, a hungry man presented with an apple by his minister is disposed to say many things. He might say "apple," "please," "fruit," "red," "God provides," "sauce," "thank you," "an apple a day . . . "

When, and only when, that first stage has happened, can the speaker respond to his altered circumstances and his own disposition to speak. The altered circumstances and various dispositions to emit Rv's serve as discriminative stimuli for him, as shown in the lower part of the preceding illustration. He can discriminate and talk about the variables affecting his disposition to speak and the Rv's that they control. For example, he might say: "I was so hungry . . . " or "This reminds me . . . " or "I was just about to pray . . . " This talking about talking is autoclitic behavior. It is somewhat *self-dependent* and includes such Rv's as "is," "is not," "except," and "all." And, it includes ordering. We will look at many examples of this process in great detail in what follows.

Now, formally and officially, AN AUTOCLITIC IS A TACT WHOSE DISCRIMINATIVE STIMULUS IS A CURRENTLY STRONG OPERANT IN THE PRIMARY VERBAL BEHAVIOR, AND WHOSE Rv IS DISCRIMINATIVE (VARIES) WITH RESPECT TO THAT OPERANT'S CONTROLLING VARIABLE, STRENGTH, OR Rv FORM.

We may say, with somewhat less rigor, that the primary verbal behavior makes likely other verbal behavior (i.e., autoclitic) that comments upon it, and also determines the order of its emission. So, when we talk we do two things. We respond to the primary variables, and to our verbal operants themselves, and we play it all out as a running commentary on what we are doing.

Notice that autoclitic operants are a special subspecies of tacts. Their discriminative stimuli are *operants*, not just Rv's, and their Rv's may serve as discriminative stimuli for intraverbals. An autoclitic is a comment on competition among operants, or the resolution of the competition, or the strength of the controlling variables, or the past history that led to those operants in the primary repertoire, and much more, which we will soon examine in some detail. But it all works like tacting, and so it isn't really very new. First, however, we should analyze some examples in detail.

KINDS OF AUTOCLITICS

Some autoclitics tact the controlling variables for primary verbal behavior. Suppose my current primary variables lead me to say, "She is in Toledo." This tells my hearer nothing about *why* I would say this. However, it may be important for my hearer to know the causes of my behavior. His reinforcement may depend on his subsequent behavior. That subsequent behavior may be very different from what it would be if my behavior was part of a textual as opposed to a tact. So I tell him, by tacting the controlling variable.

"I see by the paper (that she is in Toledo)."—A textual

"My brother says . . . "—An echoic

"I predict that . . . "—Not a simple tact, possibly an intraverbal

"I guess that . . . "—Not a tact, probably an intraverbal

Thus the primary verbal behavior remains the same, but the effect on the mediator is considerably different.

Some autoclitics tact operant strength. If the variables controlling "He is in Chicago" are functioning, the following tact their strength:

"I am sure that . . . "—Very strong

"I know that . . . "

"I suppose that . . . "—Not so strong

"I believe that . . . "

"I guess that . . . "—Not very strong

"I imagine that . . . "

"I hate to tell you this, but . . ."—Rather weak
                        because of competition

"I hesitate to say so, but . . . "

So we can see that "Hopefully, the plane will be on time" tells the hearer that the tact "the plane will be on time" was not quite strong enough to be said by itself, and to wait because some other tact may follow.

"Hopefully" is related to those autoclitics that *tact Rv competition* in the primary verbal behavior. For example, "put another way," "still," "or," "however," "although," are all Rv's that tact that another primary tact is coming up, or could have been emitted, and that if or when emitted, this next tact competes with the one that just was said.

Some Rv's have been called *quantifiers,* and this terminology is still strong in philosophical circles. Remember that in the standard philosopher's example "All swans are white," there is no discriminative stimulus for the regular tact: $S^D \to Rv$ "all swans." It is impossible to see all the swans that there are, much less all those that ever were or ever will be. Therefore, emission of the Rv "all swans" in their presence is impossible, but one can respond to his verbal behavior about swans. The next illustration shows the dynamics of this tact. The Rv "all" functionally tells the hearer that in the primary verbal behavior of the speaker, if a swan is the discriminative stimulus, "white" is going to be a Rv because of a high-strength tact. Remember, "all" is part of an autoclitic; "swan" is part of a

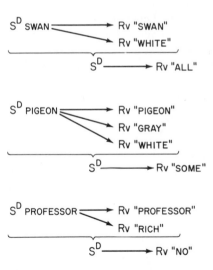

tact. The second part of the illustration shows that the Rv "some" tells the hearer that if a pigeon is the discriminative stimulus, "gray" is sometimes likely to be emitted as part of a tact. Finally, the last part of the illustration shows that "no" is part of a tact to the hearer that the speaker has no tact with a Rv "rich" for the discriminative stimulus professor. It may be said, then, that quantifiers tact the numerical properties of the relation between a controlling variable and a Rv in primary behavior.

THE AUTOCLITIC A "FUDGE FACTOR"?

To some people, this is the place where we have gone out the back door and climbed up a metaphysical tree. This whole business seems too strange to them, or strains their credulity too much. It does not seem, to some people, that an operant could be a discriminative stimulus. It does not seem to them to be a discriminable thing, some real entity that can be responded to. They argue that operants are only abstractions, and bad ones at that.

Well, I don't think that things are as bad as all that. Operants are real, public events. They are abstract, to be sure, but their members are observable, and so is the relationship between their members. Therefore, such relations may serve as the discriminative stimuli for tacts. If your operants are no secret to an outside observer, a scientist, they are no secret to you yourself. After all, you have the best access to the controlling variables that affect you and the responses that you make. So you can observe these controlling variables, tact them and tact the relations between them. And these special tacts are autoclitics.

Actually, we tact our behavior and our operants all the time, both when the behavior is verbal and when it is nonverbal. Somehow we are less surprised when a speaker tacts his nonverbal operants in a descriptive way. The top part of the next illustration shows an example of this. We often tact

$$S^D \text{ CLOCK}$$
$$S^D \text{ COAT ON}$$
$$S^D \text{ FATIGUE}$$
$$DEP^{\underline{N}}$$
$$\longrightarrow R \text{ GO HOME}$$

$$S^D \longrightarrow Rv \text{ "I WAS JUST LEAVING"}$$

$$S^D \text{ PAST VB}$$
$$+ S^D \text{ OR } DEP^{\underline{N}} \longrightarrow Rv$$

$$S^D \longrightarrow Rv \text{ "I ALWAYS SAY"}$$

$$S^D \text{ IMMINENT VB}$$
$$+ P.V.$$

$$S^D \longrightarrow Rv \text{ "I WAS ABOUT TO SAY"}$$

the behavior of nonverbal animals in a similar way. For example, we may say of a pigeon: "He is about to peck the key." When the behavior is verbal the process is exactly the same, but it appears to be somewhat different because many of the Rv's of the autoclitic vocabulary—e.g., "is," "is not," "except," "all," "no," "some,"—do not name or describe behavior. Other autoclitic Rv's do describe: "I always say . . . ," "I read that . . . ," "I was going to say . . . " The first kind of autoclitics (e.g., "all," "except") just covary with features of primary verbal behavior in conventional ways. That is all that is required; remember the nondescriptive nonnaming tacts that contain the Rv's "hello," "good morning," "phooey." These too are tacts that covary with the discriminative stimuli but don't name or describe.

We may agree that autoclitics are tacts, but then to be good scientists, we must show why they occur at all. But *we* know why they occur. The hearer needs that information (discriminative stimulus). Any Rv may be caused by more than one variable, that is, be a member of more than one operant. So the hearer must know not only what is said, but why it is said, and often he must know how strong the cause of its being said is. He needs to know this because his behavior may differ depending on what the situation is, and his subsequent reinforcement depends on the behavior he emits following the speaker's Rv. Recall our example of the man who says "oil." His hearer's future behavior is greatly determined by whether that Rv is part of a mand, a tact, an intraverbal, an echoic, or whatever. Thus the hearer reinforces the speaker for tacting his controlling variables and the strength of their control. When the speaker and the hearer are in the same skin, the hearer has just as much access to the primary variables as the speaker does; thus, and this is an empirical, testable hypothesis, when the speaker is the hearer the autoclitic commentary probably drops out. It either isn't there or, if it is, it occurs with very reduced amplitude or in an incomplete form.

Let's look at some more examples of autoclitic commentary. The next illustration shows the dynamics of *assertion* and *negation*. As soon as, but not before, the Rv's "that man" and "fat" are probable, then "is" occurs as part of a tact about the relationship between the speaker's verbal behavior and its source. It tells the hearer what the antecedent of the verbal behavior is. You say "is" when you have something to say that has a certain relationship with its antecedent, not just when something, anything, *is*. To the hearer, "is" serves as a discriminative stimulus that functions to tell him that the same discriminative stimulus is controlling both tacts, "that man" and "fat." So "is" tacts that both tacts have the same discriminative stimulus.

Once "that girl" and "fat" are likely, for some reason, if the Rv "fat" is due to some variable other than the fatness of the discriminative stimulus—perhaps an echoic, or a textual, or even an intraverbal supplementary source of strength—the speaker says "isn't." He never says

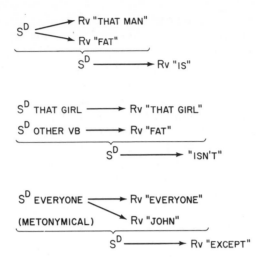

"isn't" until he is in a position to say that which is not. That is, we say "isn't" when we have something to say, not when *notness* is present. The Rv "isn't" serves as a discriminative stimulus to the hearer. It tells him that the Rv "fat" is due to some other variable than the fat of the discriminative stimulus. It is functionally equivalent to saying that "fat" is not part of a tact for "that girl."

Therefore, if everyone, that is, if all the members of a group have in the past been common accompaniments of John, then "John" is likely to be said in their presence, even if John isn't there. When this does occur, "except" may be emitted to serve as a discriminative stimulus to the hearer that "John" is not in this instance part of a tact but is being controlled by something else. That is, it tells him that "John" is likely to be due to that form of generalization that we called metonymical extension.

Other autoclitic tacts occur. I haven't given a complete list, nor will I, but here are some more examples. The Rv "and" usually occurs as part of an autoclitic that tells the hearer that there is more to come, that the speaker will speak again under the influence of the same controlling variables. The Rv "or" is a discriminative stimulus to the hearer for two or more operants in the speaker's primary verbal behavior which are both at high strength and competing. Often these operants share the same discriminative stimulus or the same Rv. A lot of *grammatical tagging* is autoclitic. Technically these are simple tacts, such as "walks," "walked," "walking." These serve as discriminative stimuli for the hearer to inform him of the temporal relationships between the controlling variables and the speaking. So it goes. Although this list is not complete, it shows the general features of the autoclitic vocabulary. Autoclitics comprise verbal behavior that doesn't happen until there is something else to say; the something else governs it. The autoclitic repertoire is talking about talking.

At this point it might be appropriate to consider a warning. A Rv may be part of an autoclitic operant in one utterance, but not be autoclitic in another. The Rv "is" may be autoclitic when the discriminative stimulus is a fat person, such as in the Rv "that man is fat." However, the same Rv, "is," cannot be autoclitic when the discriminative stimulus controlling the speaker's behavior is (1) another person's Rv (in which case the Rv is part of an echoic), (2) writing or printing (in which case the Rv is part of a textual), or (3) the speaker's own prior verbal behavior (in which case the Rv is part of an intraverbal). Examples of these follow:

(1) ECHOIC –   A: Rv "SAY THE CAKE IS GOOD"

B: S^D ——▶ Rv "THE CAKE IS GOOD"

(2) TEXTUAL– | THIS IS IT | ——▶ Rv "THIS IS IT"

(3) INTRAVERBAL

If you say the following aloud, your initial verbal behavior will be textual, but you will keep going under intraverbal control. Here are some adages:

> A stitch in time saves nine.
> Look before you leap.
> He who hesitates. . .
> A penny saved. . .

ORDERING AS AN AUTOCLITIC PROCESS

Let me remind you of the second part of the problem before us. The variables controlling primary verbal behavior often occur simultaneously, or in an order different from that of the finished speech. Now, what follows is not very intuitively acceptable for many people. We don't ordinarily tend to speak of the serial position of one Rv in a string of Rv's as one of its dimensions or behavioral properties. Nonetheless, relative temporal position (i.e., when, with respect to other Rv's, a given Rv occurs) is as much of an observable dimension as Rv form (i.e., which word, phoneme, phrase, etc., is emitted).

ORDERING IS ALSO AN AUTOCLITIC PROCESS: IT IS SIMPLY AN ALTERNATIVE TO USING THE AUTOCLITIC WORDS (RV'S SUCH AS "IS," "ALSO," "BUT"). BUT AUTOCLITIC ORDERING IS NOT AN EXCLUSIVE ALTERNATIVE TO

THE AUTOCLITIC WORDS. IT IS USED PARTLY IN PLACE OF THEM, AND PARTLY WITH THEM. ORDERING IS ITSELF A FORM OF TACTING CONTROLLED BY THE DISCRIMINATIVE STIMULI IN PRIMARY VERBAL BEHAVIOR. It depends upon operants in primary verbal behavior, just as the autoclitic words do. You don't order something unless you have something to put in order. How verbal operants are ordered depends upon themselves, upon what is to be said and why.

Remember, an autoclitic is an operant. Like all operants, it has a controlling variable and a response. One class of autoclitics has special words as the responses. The other class of autoclitics has orders of words as the responses. Even though a particular order seems like an odd sort of thing to be a response, it can be. And if it is controlled by the right sort of discriminative stimulus, it can be part of an autoclitic operant. We have particular orders as responses in nontalking behavior, as in typing from copy. Striking the keys of the typewriter in the order H I T S is a different response than striking them in the order T H I S. So, if a particular arrangement of the Rv's of the operants of primary verbal behavior covaries according to a conventional correspondence with either the controlling variables or the strength of the operants, then this arrangement fulfills the definition of autoclitic that we gave on page 129. Particular arrangements covary with particular controlling variables or strengths of operants, or competition among operants, just the way autoclitic Rv's do. Therefore, the arrangements or orderings are autoclitic too. Because they covary with events in primary verbal behavior, orderings tell the hearer something about the circumstances controlling the emission of the primary verbal Rv's. The next illustration shows the difference and great similarity between the autoclitic word solution and the autoclitic ordering solution to

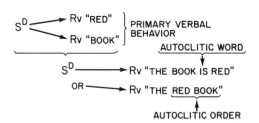

the problem of telling the hearer that the same discriminative stimulus is being tacted twice. This shows that the order of the Rv's has the same functional role and is controlled by the same variables as the Rv "is."

It might seem somewhat wasteful to have two ways of doing this. Just think of all the additional time and reinforcers that were needed. However, the next illustration shows how ordering can be a much more efficient method of tacting properties of the primary verbal behavior. If a red book is on a

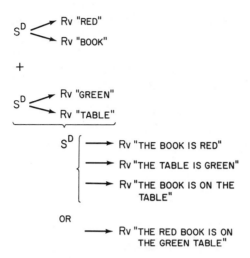

green table, the speaker has available the following Rv's at once: "red," "green," "book," "table." Thus he can say, "The book is red" and "The table is green." He can also discriminate the location of the book and say, "The book is on the table." But, instead of giving all those Rv's, including all the autoclitic ones, he uses order of Rv's, that is, "The red book is on the green table." He makes a discrimination. If *red* and *book* are both to be said (that's the discriminative stimulus), then *book* must be said after *red* (that's the autoclitic response). Of course, this doesn't always work out so nicely. Sometimes the variable controlling *book* is very strong, and therefore the conventional order breaks down somewhat and the speaker says; "The book, the red one, is on the green table, the one in the hall."

REINFORCEMENT HISTORY FOR AUTOCLITICS

What follows may be difficult for some people. I don't want to sound defensive or patronizing here. However, several people who read this book in manuscript form suggested that you be warned that this may be a place where you will have to do a lot of the work to understand. Please don't dismiss the difficulty of what follows as just lack of clarity or laziness on my part.

Other disciplines or theories of verbal behavior have been greatly impressed with the fact that speech is ordered. The principal difference between the Skinnerian and other accounts of verbal behavior is that the locus of the ordering device here is in the interrelation of primary and autoclitic operants. Because the autoclitic operants are created by conditioning, a fluent speaker must have had some reinforcement history for autoclitics.

Such a reinforcement history probably started in the way shown in the next illustration. In the earliest instances of the speaker's verbal behavior,

1. $S^D \begin{smallmatrix} \text{GREEN} \\ \text{BOOK} \end{smallmatrix}$ $\longrightarrow$ Rv "GREEN BOOK" $\longrightarrow$ S^r

2. $S^D \begin{smallmatrix} \text{RED} \\ \text{CAR} \end{smallmatrix}$ $\longrightarrow$ Rv "RED CAR" $\longrightarrow$ S^r

3. $S^D \begin{smallmatrix} \text{GOOD} \\ \text{BOY} \end{smallmatrix}$ $\longrightarrow$ Rv "GOOD BOY" $\longrightarrow$ S^r

GENERALIZED

$$S^D \Big\langle \begin{array}{l} \text{Rv OBJECT CLASS NAME} \\ \text{Rv PROPERTY CLASS NAME} \end{array}$$

$$S^D \longrightarrow \text{Rv PROPERTY-OBJECT}$$

he was presented with discriminative stimuli that had multiple properties, all of which were tactable. So he learned to tact them, usually as sound units with built-in order. For example, some children learn "all gone" as a single unitary Rv, and it takes a while before it is separable into "all" and "gone" with each under separate discriminative stimulus control. Sometimes the separation requires considerable explicit tuition. The disposition, the operant, is very strong, and *it generalizes,* as shown in the bottom part of the preceding illustration.

Now this is extremely important, especially in light of some of the criticism raised against our approach. Once the child learns a particular order, and this order generalizes; it has become autoclitic. Furthermore, all situations (discriminative stimulus combinations) need not be separately learned. Some people seem to think that autoclitics require separate conditioning for each particular Rv combination, that is, a separate reinforcement history for each of the following combinations: "good boy," "red book," "nice doggie," and so forth. That isn't so; it would take forever. We know that generalization takes care of it. Generalization is instantaneous; one reinforcement may be sufficient to get it going with widespread effects. So, if the child is effectively reinforced for "red book," or "he goes," or "if..., then...," these orderings generalize. A morphemic ordering example is provided by the child who who learned the order "up"—"er" and generalized it to "downer." Autoclitic orderings, like other conditioned responses, drop in all over the place once they have been attached to a discriminative stimulus. That's because the discriminative stimuli were all over the place all along, and once the responses are put under their control, the responses occur whenever the stimuli do.

Furthermore, *response induction* helps this process along. Remember that *response induction is the heightened probability of occurrence of responses that are similar in form to the response that was reinforced.* So, stimulus generalization allows the response of property-object order to transfer to other discriminative stimuli (property-object pairs). And the Rv form of property-object tact order tends to recur by induction. The seeming difficulty in comprehending this is due to the fact that generalization and induction are aspects of the same process in verbal behavior.

Such speed and extent of generalization and induction may seem impossible to some people. But those who do research on generalization and induction tell us that they are both very broad, widespreading processes—unless they are specifically contained by discrimination training, and even that will not wipe them out. The human organism is an especially good generalizer and inducer. This may be part of the uniqueness of primate genetic constitution. Men and monkeys are generalizers. The problem faced by educators is to teach discriminations. Pigeons and horses are great discriminators, but poor generalizers.

Other orderings are similarly acquired. Here are a few more examples. If the discriminative stimulus is an actor performing some action, the Rv's that tact the actor occur before those that tact the action, as in "the boy runs," "the girl cooks," "we study." You can draw the paradigm for this; just use the lower part of the preceding illustration as a model. Here are a couple of examples of *open frames. If* (it rains; I study; you say you will), *then* (I won't go; I get an A; I, will too). *So* (good, bright, expensive) *that* (I couldn't resist; I had to shut my eyes; I couldn't buy it).

AWARENESS

Skinner's autoclitic hypothesis is that we discriminate our own operants. However, this does not mean that we are aware that we are doing so. That is, we have no verbal behavior for which the autoclitic processes *themselves* are the controlling discriminative stimuli. If we did, we would be able to tact our autoclitic processes as they were occurring. Presumably such tacting could be taught (reinforced), but it *probably* would have to make use of nonvocal Rv's because the speech-producing muscles are busy.

This approach to the problem of awareness says that we may behave discriminatively with respect to a set of discriminative stimuli without knowing that we are doing so, or even what the relevant discriminative stimuli are. We can quite often specify the controlling variables for our behavior, as in "I'm having three superburgers because I haven't had breakfast or lunch''; "I said 'it's raining' because it is, that's why.'' Quite often we cannot, though. You can see some nonverbal examples when you try to specify the variables that control your walking, or riding a bicycle. You cannot tell someone how to do it. Another somewhat more verbal example is provided by my wife. To claim that she talks without awareness of what she is saying would be too risky for me. However, she was able to engage in a highly skilled discriminated form of verbal behavior without knowing how she did it or what the discriminative stimuli for her behavior were. Furthermore, she was taught this behavior without having the discriminative stimuli named or described for her. This all came about in the following manner.

After her father had quit the rodeo circuit as a performer, he was asked to judge several events. With the passage of time and many more rodeos, he gained a reputation as a good judge of cutting horses. His ability to judge these animals came in part from his experience as a rider of them in rodeos and in part from his experience as a working rancher. *Cutting horses* are specially trained animals used by cowboys in selecting a cow or a steer from a group and cutting it out of the herd, thereby isolating it from the rest of the cattle so that it may be tied or branded or whatever. Because of the importance of these operations in practical ranch work, cutting horse events are of great interest to serious ranchers and rodeo attenders. When my wife was about ten years old she began to sit with her father while he officiated as a judge of cutting horse contests, and soon she began to keep score, albeit unofficially. At the end of each horse and rider's performance, she would compare her estimate of the performance with that of the official judge, her father. After a few years and a number of rodeos, she was able to develop judgments that agreed with his within one or two points. Generally both she and her father would assign the same score to a contestant.

So, here we have an example of verbal behavior, the assigning of a score to a horse and rider, which is based upon a highly complex series of discriminative stimuli, the performance of the man and the animal, which was learned without explicit tuition, and which cannot be described by the behaver herself. That is, even to this day my wife can judge cutting horse performances, but cannot say what cues she uses, nor can she tell me what to look for. She can also tell me from what sort of animal the farmer took the natural fertilizer as we drive past the field, but she cannot tell me what discriminative stimuli differentiate the odor of horse versus cow dung. You and I don't specialize in discriminating odors, but perfume chemists do. They can be trained to speak in response to the discriminative stimuli that govern their behavior and to tact them with some degree of precision, just as the soil expert can learn to tact the discriminative stimuli that govern his behavior in identifying fertilizers. Once this is done, the door is open to the explicit verbal tuition of others in the same skills.

Slips of the tongue are caused but often pass unnoticed. As I have said before, a good way to find these is to listen to recordings. Another good source is a classroom lecturer. If, instead of trying to write it down, you pay attention to what the professor is saying and how he is saying it, you will hear all sorts of intrusions and distortions. You can often discover their probable causes. But notice, the speaker usually discriminates neither his controlling variables nor his Rv's, because he does not recognize that he is misspeaking. Sometimes he does and "corrects himself," but this self-editing occurs much less frequently than one might imagine if one has not studied tape recordings. In general, then, awareness presents no difficulties for the autoclitic explanation of verbal behavior.

Other more highly verbal examples abound, too. A somewhat esoteric one is *automatic writing*. The writer's hand, pen, and paper may be concealed from his eyes by an elevated board. He answers questions by writing but may read an interesting story or carry on a conversation with the experimenter on some other topic. Often the subject doesn't know that he has written anything, much less what he has written or why. Thus, he produces verbal behavior, albeit written verbal behavior, without any awareness of the discriminative stimuli by which his behavior is controlled, or the Rv's that he emits.

Leon Solomons and Gertrude Stein published one of the earliest papers on this topic in the *Psychological Review* in 1896, and B. F. Skinner wrote an article in the *Atlantic Monthly* in 1934 pointing out the great similarities of style and content in Miss Stein's 1896 paper and her later literary works, especially *Tender Buttons*. He claimed that these similarities indicated that she had written her novels by the automatic writing process. Here are the three samples of Miss Stein's automatic writing that were included in the 1896 paper:

1. Hence there is no possible way of avoiding what I have spoken of, and if this is not believed by the people of whom you have spoken, then it is not possible to prevent the people of whom you have spoken so glibbly. . .

2. When he could not be the longest and thus to be, and thus to be, the strongest.

3. This long time when he did this best time, and he could thus have been bound, and in this long time, when he could be this to first use of this long time. . .

Miss Stein became so good at automatic writing "that distraction by reading was almost unnecessary. Miss Stein found it sufficient distraction often to simply read what her arm wrote, but following three or four words behind her pencil."

Let us now look at some samples from *Tender Buttons*. At this point an aside is in order. Skinner's argument is much more complex than the comparison of the samples of Miss Stein's automatic writing.

1. A table means does it not my dear it means a whole steadiness. Is it likely that a change.
   A table means more than a glass even a looking glass is tall. A table means necessary places and a revision a revision of a little thing it means it does mean that there has been a stand, a stand where it did shake.
2. China is not down when there are plates, lights are not ponderous and incalculable.
3. **Roast Beef**

   In the inside there is sleeping, in the outside there is reddening, in the morning there is meaning, in the evening there is feeling. In the evening there is feeling. In feeling anything is resting, in feeling anything is mounting, in feeling there is resignation, in feeling there is recognition, in feeling there is recurrence and entirely mistaken there is pinching. All the standards have streamers and all the curtains have bed linen and all the yellow has discrimination and all the circle has circling. This makes sand. [Paragraph one of a 36 paragraph poem by Miss Stein.]

Miss Stein denied Skinner's claim, and a host of literary people objected vigorously to Skinner's article. Perhaps they were worried that the explanation took the "art" out of the product. Judith Thurman recently continued the literati's protest against Skinner's analysis. And she reprinted "Roast Beef"! I have to agree with Skinner, who wrote that it was unfortunate that Miss Stein published this stuff, for it detracted from her other more valuable work. Automatic writing is not art. It is no more art than samples of the various orders of approximation to English. Here are some samples of those collected by Miller and Selfridge:

1. they saw the play Saturday and sat down beside him
2. road in the country was insane especially in dreary rooms where they have some books to buy for studying Greek
3. go it will be pleasant to you when I am near the table in the dining room was crowded with people it crashed into were screaming that they had been
4. house to ask for is to earn our living by working towards a goal for his team in old New-York was a wonderful place wasn't it even pleasant to talk about and laugh hard when he tells lies he should not tell me the reason why you are is evident.

In his "Creating the Creative Artist," Skinner observed that the creative artist is an expert in variation and selection. The variations (original idea, themes, materials, treatments) come from many sources. The experimental analyst of behavior has no access to these, so he cannot tell us about them. But the creative artist usually has no verbal repertoire for the sources either. He hasn't been reinforced for tacting them, so he is unaware of them too. The book *Anna Livia Plurabelle: The Making of a Chapter,* edited by Higgenson, shows that Joyce did just what Skinner claimed. *Finnegans Wake* easily has the complexity and in parts the redundancy and ambiguity of Miss

Stein's automatic writing, but it is art and it is successful (reinforcing to both the writer and the reader).

This has been a long digression, but I have strong verbal behavior "about" all this. Incidentally, it is interesting to see that Skinner was an object of scorn to the humanists even at the beginning of his career. But more important for us is the fact that Miss Stein's automatic writing shows that significant verbal behavior may be produced by discriminative stimuli of which the behaver is not aware. And, the behaver may also be unaware of his responses until he examines them at a later time.

12

some
implications

We are in the homestretch now. All that remains is to apply what we know to some problems that have greatly concerned the traditional analysts of speech and verbal behavior.

THE HEARER

First, let us pull the hearer together, so to speak. We have discussed him at various times in the preceding chapters, but we have largely concentrated on the speaker. It is now appropriate to put the hearer side of the fluent speaker-hearer in perspective. This is mostly just a resume of what we have said before. *The hearer has two major roles.*

His first major mode of functioning is as *stimulus generator.* He does this in two ways. WHEN HE PRODUCES STIMULI AFTER A SPEAKER RESPONDS; WE CALL HIM A REINFORCEMENT MEDIATOR. Without him, the response reinforcer relation does not exist; and without that, operants cannot be created or maintained. In his role of mediator, he behaves slightly differently for each class of controlling variables for the speaker's operants. He must discriminate among controlling variable Rv relationships affecting the speaker in order to reinforce appropriately. WHEN THE HEARER PROVIDES STIMULI BEFORE THE SPEAKER BEGINS TO SPEAK, WE CALL HIM AN AUDIENCE. Here he functions as a discriminative stimulus and shows up in address and as a variable which helps select among Rv's and audibility in a supplementary way.

The hearer's other major role is as a *stimulus receiver*. AS A HEARER PER SE HIS BEHAVIOR IS PRINCIPALLY ECHOIC; HE LISTENS. THAT IS, LISTENING IS COMPOSED OF ECHOIC BEHAVIOR. Usually this echoic behavior is covert, but it can be, and sometimes is, overt. Listening, or hearing, is not just stimulus absorption. It is not merely a passive transaction between the ear and the brain via the organ of Corti and the tympanic nerve. The hearer of speech does things as he listens, and his doing things is part of his hearing and necessary to it.

Speakers have their behavior modified by the hearer's activities, and their behavior reflects this. Effective speakers talk at rates that are conducive to echoism: not too fast, or there wouldn't be enough time for the hearer to echo; and not too slow so as to prevent the hearer from starting on intraverbals which might interfere with his echoing the speaker. Especially in dramatic speaking or emotional exhortations, the pace of speech must be varied so that some words (Rv's) may elicit emotional respondents, and the elicited responses may then subside. Remember, a stimulus may serve as a discriminative stimulus for several operant responses, and also serve as a CS for other respondent behaviors. For example, the rat's visual food pellet may serve as a discriminative stimulus for operant seizing and chewing as well as a CS for respondent salivation.

Appropriate rates of speaking are selectively reinforced by the hearer. This is generally done by termination of negative conditioned reinforcers. Sometimes punishment is applied when the speaker responds at rates that are not conducive to the hearer's echoing. For example:

"Hurry up; don't take all day."

"Get on with it, man."

"Slow down; you talk too fast."

"Take it easy."

"Relax, I won't go away."

The hearer does this so that he can echo and in some cases produce intraverbals. If the stimuli produced by the speaker change too fast, the hearer cannot do that. If the stimulus flow is too slow, it is aversive to the hearer. In the latter case he has to mark time with behavior that will set off chains or clusters of intraverbals which are competitors for what is to be echoed next. This is, of course, related to UNDERSTANDING, WHICH IS OUR ABILITY TO ECHO AND USE OUR ECHOIC Rv'S AS DISCRIMINATIVE STIMULI FOR OUR INTRAVERBAL BEHAVIOR WHICH LEADS ULTIMATELY TO OUR REIN-

FORCEMENT. As an example of this we may consider the advice case. In understanding we echo the speaker, which provides us with Rv's that can serve as discriminative stimuli for us later, such as how to go to the store, what to do to prepare for the test, how to lose friends and antagonize in-laws. Thus, the hearer modulates the speaker's rate to produce a speed that is most conducive to his own understanding (echoing).

This view of what the hearer does is a variant of what are called the *motor theories of speech perception.* There are several versions of those theories and some have greater or lesser commitments to peripheralism. We needn't go into them here. We may note, however, that an interesting implication of some of them is that a person cannot remember the sound of a speaker or a musical instrument unless he can make it himself.

MEANING

Earlier I said that meaning is not a natural science property of any word. Meaning is not a publicly measurable dimension of a Rv, nor are any of the traditional philosophical notions such as reference, connotation, or denotation. Meaning is, so to speak, added on without changing the response topography or the stimulus dimensions of a Rv. Therefore, to find the meaning of a word, we have to look at things other than just which word, or sequence of sounds, occurred, because the meaning is not carried by the word itself.

According to the Skinnerian analysis we have been exploring, THE MEANING OF A Rv, WHICH MANY BE LARGER OR SMALLER THAN A WORD, IS GIVEN BY POINTING TO THE DISCRIMINATIVE STIMULI OF WHICH IT IS A FUNCTION AND/OR BY POINTING TO THE Rv'S FOR WHICH THE Rv IN QUESTION IS AN INTRAVERBAL DISCRIMINATIVE STIMULUS. Thus the meaning of the Rv "hat" is given by pointing to the discriminative stimuli for that Rv, such as an object, a text, overheard speech, "coat" in the speaker's preceding speech. However, our exposition of the meaning is not complete until we give the Rv's for which "hat" is an intraverbal discriminative stimulus, such as "an article of apparel worn on the head," "clothing," "wool," "ear flaps." Thus, a *word* has *full* or *complete* meaning if there are discriminative stimuli for that word as a Rv, and if that word serves as a discriminative stimulus for other Rv's. But not all Rv's have these properties, as we shall see.

MEANINGLESS WORDS (Rv'S) ARE THOSE FOR WHICH THERE ARE NO DISCRIMINATIVE STIMULI EXCEPT TEXTUAL OR ECHOIC ONES, AND WHICH ALSO SERVE AS DISCRIMINATIVE STIMULI FOR NO INTRAVERBALS. Ebbinghaus tried to make little words of this sort; he called them nonsense syllables. If I say "miv" to you, I have given you an echoic antecedent, and as you read it, the controlling variable for your speaking is a text. But notice that nothing else would do as a discriminative stimulus. As much research has shown, however, nonsense syllables do control some intraverbals, and some tacts, for example, "a nonsense syllable," "three letter," "miffed," "shiv," "quivver." So, to the extent that there are any such operants for which "miv" is the discriminative stimulus, they constitute its meager meaning.

AMBIGUITY OCCURS WHEN THE RV COULD BE CONTROLLED BY MORE THAN ONE DISCRIMINATIVE STIMULUS AND SERVES AS THE DISCRIMINATIVE STIMULUS FOR MORE THAN ONE RV, AND THE HEARER HAS NO ACCESS TO THE CIRCUMSTANCES CONTROLLING THE SPEAKER'S BEHAVIOR. Examples are legion:

"She didn't marry him because of his money."

"They are eating apples."

"The mad scientist's female robot developed a short in her wiring and wanted to marry him, but he refused her."

In each case the utterance is ambiguous as a stimulus to the hearer, but it is not ambiguous as a response; the speaker *knows* because he has access to the variables controlling his speech. Ambiguity is a "linguistic problem" only if we consider a word to be the same thing no matter when or why it occurs. By giving a functional account of verbal behavior, we have no problem, because for us the cause of a Rv helps define it.

An analysis of speaking that is similar to the one we have been looking at was given by Bertrand Russell in his book *My Philosophical Development:*

> A word is used "correctly" when the average hearer will be affected by it in the way intended. This is a psychological, not a literary, definition of "correctness." The literary definition would substitute, for the average hearer, "a person of high education living a long time ago"; the purpose of this definition is to make it difficult to speak or write correctly.

> * * *

> Philosophers and bookish people generally tend to live a life dominated by words, and even to forget that it is the essential function of words to have a connection of one sort or another with facts, which are in general nonlinguistic. Some modern philosophers have gone so far as to say that words should never be confronted with facts but should live in a pure, autonomous world where they are compared only with other words. . . . These authors tell us that the attempt to confront language with fact is "metaphysics" and is on this ground to be condemned. This is one of those views which are so absurd that only very learned men could possibly adopt them.

THINKING

In traditional, commonsense accounts, *thinking* is a preverbal activity of some sort. Thinking is said to be "having thoughts or ideas which are usually words or images," or else to be "taking place in the mind" (according to old- and new-fashioned mentalists). Or else thinking is supposedly "what goes on in the brain" (according to those who are somewhere in between). And some merely say that "thinking is what words express." I have not said or implied anything of that sort here. So far I have claimed that verbal behavior is nothing but a function of past history and current circumstances of the speaker-hearer.

There are several problems with a view of thinking as a cause of verbal behavior. The behavioristic tradition has been to deny everything about thinking. Watson, who started behaviorism as an "ism," did just that. He said something on the order of the following. Thought, ideas, and images are not the subject matter of science; they are metaphysical constructions, not data; furthermore, the brain is the subject of another discipline, or at least physiological psychology, and neither physiology nor physiological psychology tells us anything about thoughts.

That is just too easy, a cop-out.

A modern behaviorist has only one real problem. It is incontrovertible that people do say such things as "I am thinking," or "I have an idea," or "I see the image of..." The problem is, then, to say what controls this behavior and how it got control. The modern behaviorist rejects traditional views that ascribe thought to processes that occur before speech, because these theories of *thinking* don't describe what we do. When talking, we don't stop and think very much, if at all. It is also hard to see how we learned to tact our mental states or brain processes. Remember, to reinforce accurate tacting, the reinforcement mediator must have access to the discriminative stimulus to be put in control of the Rv, so that the reinforcement may be dispensed only when there is an exact conventional correspondence between the discriminative stimulus and the Rv. How does a mediator look into your head when teaching you to say, "I am thinking"?

No matter how hard it is for the preverbal activity views of thinking to account for these difficulties, obviously "thinking," "image," and "idea" as Rv's are parts of tacts for something. The occurrence of these Rv's is lawfully controlled by some states of affairs. Thought may not be a preverbal cause of speech in the traditional sense, but something is being tacted. The modern behaviorist must tell what it is that is being tacted, where it is, and how the tacts were established.

Let us proceed at once to where I believe a fully informed functional analysis of the Rv "thinking" and allied Rv's such as "image" and "idea" would take us. The principal hypothesis is as follows.

Rv's such as "thinking," and related Rv's such as "image" or "idea," are parts of tacts controlled by any behavior whose effect is principally upon the behaver himself. This behavior is not itself directly reinforced, but it produces controlling variables for other behavior which is reinforced. We call such behavior THINKING. Thinking is caused by real muscle movements, not just the brain or nervous system. It may be verbal or nonverbal, overt or covert. The stimuli arising from such behavior give rise to the phenomenology of thought or mental life. But these phenomenological aspects are a consequence of action—its accompaniment, not its cause.

This hypothesis implies that some discriminative stimuli—for example, a problem such as How do I get from here to downtown? or How do I fill up this time in which I have nothing to do?—provide the occasion for behavior whose principal outcome is to stimulate further behavior, that is, to arouse a solution or fill the boring interval of time. So, on some occasions a discriminative stimulus starts off a sequence such as $R_1:S^D \rightarrow R_2:S^D \rightarrow R_3:S^D \rightarrow R_4:S^D \rightarrow R \rightarrow S^R$ where responses 1 to 4 have as their principal effects the stimulation of the next response in the sequence. Most of the time we just run off this behavior without comment. Sometimes, however, we have some Rv's for which this sequence, or ones like it, serve as a discriminative stimuli; that is, when we say we are "thinking."

Responses in thinging may be *covert*; it certainly is more economical, saving time and energy, to have them that way. They may be *overt* if the behavior is not well conditioned, or the punishment for errors is severe, or the environment around the behaver is noisy. They may be *verbal*. I am thinking as I write this, not just before. Finally, they may be *nonverbal,* as when a child ties a string around his finger, or a man puts his wallet and watch in a certain place on his dresser top prior to going to bed. Therefore, according to the hypothesis presented here, writing notes to one's self, reading them, and putting things out to remind one to do something are all part of thinking. Does the rat that runs in a wheel to turn on a bar, which delivers a pellet of food when he presses it, think? He is on a chain schedule of reinforcement, but do chain schedules constitute thinking? Probably not—mainly because the rat's behavior is primarily effective on the external environment. His bar-pressing and wheel-turning are necessary to produce environmental changes in which further responding may be reinforced. This is not the case with most of what we call thinking. The environment does not have to be prepared or altered by thinking in order that the terminal response be made or reinforced. No environmental contingencies require looking at a map before getting on a bus. You don't have to look at the paper in order to put your foot on the step. But the map reading is thinking.

Let us look at the various kinds of thinking in somewhat greater detail.

Before we do this, I want to facilitate matters by engaging in a brief digression on covert behavior.

Remember that RESPONSE INDUCTION IS A PROCESS THAT PRODUCES RESPONSE TOPOGRAPHIES THAT DIFFER FROM THOSE THAT WERE REINFORCED. If reinforcement is repeated, and the mediator is not stringent about particular values of the intensive dimensions of responding, then the modal value of various intensive dimensions tends to drift off toward the least effortful. Therefore, as a result of reinforcement of overt instances of behavior, some covert responses of the same form, but smaller magnitude, may become more probable. Such responses are still very much parts of operants, very much due to reinforcement, and still observable by outsiders if they have amplifying equipment. The responses are available to the insider, the behaver himself. He has direct access to them via his internal receptors.

Another principle should also be recalled now. A chain may be kept going, sustained, by proprioceptive stimuli alone. Subsequent behavior may be made a function of prior behavior; each R may provide the discriminative stimulus for the succeeding one. If there are no *exteroceptive* (outside the skin) stimuli, such response-produced discriminative stimuli may be the only ones to sustain the behavior chain. Many experiments with *tandem* schedules of reinforcement (chains with no exteroceptive discriminative stimuli) show that this is the case. I won't review them here; they are discussed in the book by Ferster and Skinner.

Hence we may conclude that covert chains may occur, and that these may constitute the major part of what we tact when saying "thinking." This is a *hypothesis*. But, it is not making use of *hypothetical constructs*, that is, events, entities, or processes occurring somewhere else or in some other discipline's data language, such as physiology. All the elements of this hypothesis are real and within the data language of psychology. A formal statement of the hypothesis is as follows. MANY SO-CALLED MENTAL ACTS ARE COVERT BEHAVIOR CHAINS; THE AWARENESS THAT ACCOMPANIES THEM IS DUE TO THE INTEROCEPTIVE STIMULI GENERATED BY THE COVERT BEHAVIOR.

Now we may fully consider some examples of when people "think."

Sometimes the behavior is *covert verbal behavior*. This was Watson's solution to the problem of where thinking was. He restricted the mind to the windpipe. Many opponents of behavioristic analyses of language and cognition suppose all behaviorists are still back in the 1920's holding on to the Watsonian analysis. Well, such muscle-produced movements aren't restricted to those of the vocal cords. The vocal musculature—the muscles involved in producing speech—is extremely extensive and complex. It involves many of the muscles of the head and chest. Electrical recordings from the muscles themselves, called *electromyography,* show increased activity during the solving of verbal problems in reasoning and arithmetic. If the subject is a deaf-mute who knows sign language, however, the activity is not in his vocal musculature, but in his fingers.

Covert nonverbal behavior has been recorded when subjects were asked to imagine seeing the Eiffel Tower. It appeared in the eye muscles. If they were asked to imagine lifting a suitcase, it appeared in the arm, shoulder, and back muscles. Surprisingly, a lot of these studies were done a long time ago. Reports of many of these older experiments on covert behavior have been compiled by McGuigan (albeit the book by McGuigan and Schoonover reports much of the more recent work), who also discusses the problems and issues involved in collecting data on these events.

Overt nonverbal thinking occurs in many places. For example, overt nonverbal thinking occurs in sleep during those stages in which rapid eye movements (REM's) occur. Some investigators have found reasonably good correlations between the patterns of the eye movements and the content of the imagery of the dream. Overt nonverbal thinking occurs during examinations in school. At the University of Minnesota, all exams in psychology are multiple choice and use machine-scored answer sheets that require only blacking in a circle. Yet the question papers are frequently covered with drawings and erasures. I mentioned some other nonverbal overt thinking in talking about a man's preretiring routine.

Finally, plenty of *overt verbal thinking* occurs. Children do a great deal of it; you can observe it happening if you remain concealed from them. Professors do it too. In class, especially when I lecture, I listen to what I say, *usually*. My listening is not preverbal; it is simultaneous with my speaking. If I misspeak and don't hear and correct myself, students say, "He isn't thinking about what he is saying." Sometimes it seems that the principal effect of my behavior in that situation is entirely upon me. So, on these occasions I am thinking as I talk. It is not preverbal, but verbal and completely overt.

I said that the behaviorists' original problem was to explain what is being tacted when a man says that he is "thinking." Now we can see that when he says "I am thinking" he is just tacting his behavior whose principal effect is on himself. We do tact our overt behavior, as in "I am opening the door." Hence, we can tact both our overt and covert behavior, as in "I am thinking" (I am behaving so as to stimulate myself to further reinforced behavior).

This motor theory of thought is old and, surprisingly, still good; it has never been refuted. Its name is *peripheralism*. Its principal rival is *centralism*, which is shown paradigmatically in the top part of the next illustration. CENTRALISM, WHICH IS THE MOST WIDELY ACCEPTED THEORY TODAY, HOLDS THAT ONCE THE CENTRAL NERVOUS SYSTEM IS STARTED OFF BY SOME OUTSIDE EVENT, SAY A DISCRIMINATIVE STIMULUS, AUTONOMOUS BRAIN PROCESSES (BP) ARE ALL THAT ARE NECESSARY AND SUFFICIENT FOR WHAT HAS TRADITIONALLY BEEN CALLED THINKING. That is, centralists say that the brain can drive itself; one brain process (BP) can set off the next, and this the next, and so on, until finally some state of the brain causes an overt

CENTRALISM:
$$S^D \nearrow BP \rightarrow BP \rightarrow BP \rightarrow BP \searrow Rv \rightarrow S^r$$

PERIPHERALISM:
$$S^D \nearrow BP \searrow R:S^D \nearrow BP \searrow R:S^D \nearrow BP \searrow Rv \rightarrow S^r$$
$$S^D \rightarrow R:S^D \rightarrow R:S^D \rightarrow Rv \rightarrow S^r$$

response. Moreover, centralists say that the brain is spontaneously active, that it can initiate a train of processes *ab initio*.

Observe carefully that the PERIPHERALISTS' POSITION DOES NOT DENY THE EXISTENCE OR NECESSITY OF CENTRAL NERVOUS SYSTEM ACTION IN THINKING. IT, AS DEPICTED IN THE LOWER PART OF THE ILLUSTRATION, ARGUES THAT BRAIN PROCESSES ARE BY THEMSELVES NOT SUFFICIENT FOR THINKING. THE PERIPHERALISTS CONTEND THAT AN ADDITIONAL NECESSARY FACTOR IS PERIPHERAL EVENTS, THAT IS, STIMULI ARISING FROM REAL MUSCLE-PRODUCED MOVEMENTS.

Unfortunately, the way to decide which of these two positions is correct is conceptually clear, but technically impossible. If we could show that a completely paralyzed person or a brain in a jar could think, then we would know that peripheralism is wrong. Suppose we were able to keep the brain of a man alive in a jar, as in the science fiction stories. Then we could give it an arithmetic or a geometry problem to do. It would have to be a problem we were sure it didn't know the solution of but did have the information to solve. Then, if we removed all external stimulation sources for a while, say half an hour, and then reconnected the communication machinery, we could see if it had the solution. If it did, and the process was repeatable with new problems, and it could tell us what it did while it was disconnected, then we would know that peripheralism is wrong and centralism is correct. Because that experiment hasn't been done, peripheralism is still a viable alternative, and it is consistent with all data we have at this time.

We have completed our exercise. We see now that a complete scientific account of why a man says what he says when he says it can be given. This account made no appeal to events, entities, or processes somewhere outside the domain of stimuli or responses. Minds and brains, grammars and intentions, ideas and cognitions, have been shown unnecessary for a complete, causal, naturalistic account. Man himself has been eliminated as a causal variable; he is just a place where causal variables interact to produce talking.

suggestions
for further reading

For an introduction to research by Skinner and his followers, see the books by

Holland and Skinner
Honig
Keller and Schoenfeld
Reese
Reynolds

Also see Skinner's books

The Behavior of Organisms
Science and Human Behavior
The Technology of Teaching
Contingencies of Reinforcement
Verbal Behavior

Skinner's views on scientific method are stated in the above and in

Beyond Freedom and Dignity

Cumulative Record
About Behaviorism

Advanced work in Skinnerian research continues and is reported in books by Ferster and Skinner, Honig, and Hendry, for example. The *Journal of the Experimental Analysis of Behavior* and the *Journal of Applied Behavior Analysis* regularly publish several thousand pages of reports of research in the Skinnerian tradition each year.

references

Allen G.W. *William James; a biography.* New York: Viking, 1967.

Bloomfield, L. *Language.* New York: Holt, 1933.

Bousfield, W. A. The occurrence of clustering in the recall of randomly arranged associates. *Journal of General Psychology,* 1953, 49, 229-40.

Bruce, D. J. Effects of context upon intelligibility of heard speech. In C. Cherry (ed.), *Information theory; papers read at a symposium on 'information theory' held at the Royal Institution, London, September 12th to 16th 1955,* pp. 245-52. London: Butterworths, 1956.

Bryant, M. M., and Aiken, J. R. *Psychology of English.* New York: Columbia University Press, 1940.

Carroll, L. pseudonym of C. L. Dodgson. *Alice's adventures in wonderland.* London: Macmillan, 1865.

Davenport, D. Bee language. *Science,* 1974, 186, 975.

De Laguna, G. *Speech: Its function and development.* Bloomington: University of Indiana Press, 1927, 1963.

Ebbinghaus, H. *Über das gedächtnis.* Leipzig: Dunker & Humblot, 1885. Reissued as *Memory: A contribution to experimental psychology,* trans. H. A. Ruger and C. E. Bussenius. New York: Dover, 1964.

Ervin, S. M. Language and TAT content in bilinguals. *Journal of Abnormal and Social Psychology,* 1964, 68, 500-507.

Estes, K. W. Some effects of reinforcement upon verbal behavior of children. Unpublished doctoral dissertation, University of Minnesota, 1945.

Estes, W. K. Learning. *Annual Review of Psychology,* 1956, 7, 1-38.

Ferster, C. B., and Skinner, B. F. *Schedules of reinforcement.* New York: Appleton-Century-Crofts, 1957.

Findley, J. D. An experimental outline for building and exploring multi-operant behavior repertoires. *Journal of the Experimental Analysis of Behavior,* 1962, 5, 113-66.

Foley, J. P., Jr., and Macmillan, Z. Mediated generalization and the interpretation of verbal behavior: V. 'Free association' as related to differences in professional training *Journal of Experimental Psychology,* 1943, 33, 299-310.

Frisch, K. v. *Dance language and orientation of bees.* Cambridge, Mass.: Harvard University Press, 1967.

Frisch, K. v., Wenner, A. M., and Johnson, D. L. Honeybees: Do they use direction and distance information provided by their dancers? *Science,* 1967, 158, 1072-77.

Galton, F. *Inquiries into human faculty and its development.* London: Macmillan, 1883.

Gardner, R. A., and Gardner, B. T. Teaching sign language to a chimpanzee. Science, 1969, 165, 664-72.

Goodenough, F. L. Semantic choice and personality structure. *Science,* 1946, 104, 451-56.

Greenspoon, J. The reinforcing effect of two spoken sounds on the frequency of two responses. *American Journal of Psychology,* 68, 409-16.

Guthrie, E. R. *The psychology of learning.* New York: Harper, 1935.

Hahn, E. A reporter at large: Washoese. *New Yorker,* 11 December 1971, 47, 54-98.

Hale, H. *Ethnography and philology.* Philadelphia: Lea and Blanchard, 1846. Ridgewood, N.J.: Gregg Press, 1968.

Hanson, N. R. Discussion. In M. Radner and S.Winokur (eds.), *Analyses of theories and methods of physics and psychology; Minnesota studies in the philosophy of science,* Vol. IV, p. 243. Minneapolis: University of Minnesota Press, 1970.

Hayman, D. (ed.). *A first-draft version of Finnegans Wake.* Austin: University of Texas Press, 1963.

Hendry, D. P. *Conditioned reinforcement.* Homewood, Ill.: Dorsey, 1969.

Higginson, F. H. (ed.). *Anna Livia Plurabelle: The making of a chapter.* Minneapolis: University of Minnesota Press, 1960.

Hildum, D. C.. and Brown, R. W. Verbal reinforcement and interviewer bias. *Journal of Abnormal and Social Psychology,* 1956, 53, 108-11.

Hoijer, H. The Sapir-Whorf hypothesis. In H. Hoijer (ed.), *Language in culture,* pp. 92-105. Chicago: University of Chicago Press, 1954.

Holland, J. G., and Skinner, B. F. *The analysis of behavior.* New York: McGraw-Hill, 1961.

Holz, W. C., and Azrin, N. H. Conditioning human verbal behavior. In W. K. Honig (ed.), *Operant behavior: Areas of research and application,* pp. 790-826. Englewood Cliffs, NJ: Prentice-Hall, Inc., 1966.

Homans, G. C. *Social behavior: Its elementary forms* (rev. ed.). New York: Harcourt, Brace & Jovanovich, 1974.

Honig, W. K. (ed.). *Operant behavior: Areas of research and application.* Englewood Cliffs, NJ: Prentice-Hall, Inc., 1966.

Howes, D., and Osgood, C. E. On the combination of associative probabilities in linguistic contexts. *American Journal of Psychology,* 1954, 67, 241-58.

Hull, C. L. *Principles of behavior.* Englewood Cliffs, NJ: Prentice-Hall, Inc., 1943.

Irwin, O. C. Infant speech. *Scientific American,* 1949, 181, 22-24.

Jakobson, R. *Studies on child language and aphasia.* The Hague: Mouton, 1971.

Jakobson, R., Fant, C. G. M., and Halle, M. *Preliminaries to speech analysis: The distinctive features and their correlates.* Cambridge, Mass.: M.I.T. Press, 1951, 1952, 1961, 1963, 1967.

Jenkins, J. J., and Russell, W. A. Associative clustering during recall. *Journal of Abnormal and Social Psychology,* 1952, 47, 818-21.

Jesperson, O. *Language: Its nature, development and origin.* London: George Allen & Unwin, 1922.

Johnson, D. L. Honeybees: Do they use the direction information contained in their dance maneuver? *Science,* 1967, 155, 844-47.

Joyce, J. *Finnegans wake.* New York: Viking, 1939.

Judson, A. J., and Cofer, C. N. Reasoning as an associative process. I. Direction as a simple verbal problem. *Psychological Reports,* 1956, 2, 469-76.

Kagan, J., and Haveman, E. *Psychology: An introduction.* 2nd ed. New York: Harcourt, Brace & Jovanovich, 1972.

Kaplan, E. L., and Kaplan, G. The prelinguistic child. In J. Eliot (ed.), *Human development and cognitive processes,* pp. 358-81. New York: Holt, Rinehart & Winston, 1971.

Keller, F. S., and Schoenfeld, W. N. *Principles of psychology: A systematic text in the science of behavior.* Englewood Cliffs, NJ: Prentice-Hall, Inc., 1950.

Kent, G. H., and Rosanoff, A. J. A study of association in insanity. *American Journal of Insanity,* 1910, 67, 37-96, 317-90.

Lorenz, K. *Studies in animal and human behavior,* 2 vols. Cambridge, Mass.: Harvard University Press, 1970, 1971.

McGuigan, F. J. *Thinking: Studies of covert language processes.* Englewood Cliffs, NJ: Prentice-Hall, 1966.

McGuigan, F. J., and Schoonover, R. A. (eds.). *The psychophysiology of thinking: Studies of covert processes.* New York: Academic, 1973.

McNeil, E. B. Dependency: The egg hardens when the butter melts. *Contemporary Psychology,* 1960, 5, 390-92.

Mednick, M. T. Mediated generalization and the incubation effect as a function of manifest anxiety. *Journal of Abnormal and Social Psychology,* 1957, 55, 315-21.

Miller, G. A. *Language and communication.* New York: McGraw-Hill, 1951.

Miller, G. A., and Selfridge, J. A. Verbal context and the recall of meaningful material. *American Journal of Psychology,* 1950, 63, 176-85.

Palermo, D. S., and Jenkins, J. J. *Word-association norms: Grade school through college.* Minneapolis: University of Minnesota Press, 1964.

Palmer, A. S. *Folk-etymology, a dictionary of verbal corruptions or words perverted in form or meaning, by false derivation or mistaken analogy.* London: G. Bell, 1882.

Post, E. L. *Emily Post's etiquette.* 12th rev. ed. New York: Funk & Wagnalls, 1969.

Premack, D. A functional analysis of language. *Journal of the Experimental Analysis of Behavior,* 1970, 14, 107-25.

Reese, E. P. *Experiments in operant behavior.* New York: Appleton-Century-Crofts, 1964.

Reynolds, G. S. *A primer of operant conditioning.* Glenview, Ill.: Scott, Foresman, 1968.

Rosenthal, R. *Experimenter effects in behavioral research.* New York: Naiburg Publishing Corp., 1966.

Russell, B. *My philosophical development.* New York: Simon & Schuster, 1959. ©1959 by George Allen & Unwin Ltd.

Sapir, E. *Abnormal types of speech in Nootka.* Canada, Geological Survey, Memoir 62, Anthropological Series No. 5. Ottawa: Government Printing Bureau, 1915. Reprinted in *Selected writings of Edward Sapir in language, culture, and personality,* pp. 179-96. Berkeley: University of California Press, 1949.

Sapir, E. Male and female forms of speech in Yana. In St. W. J. Teeuwen (ed.), *Donum Natalicium Schrijnen.* Utrecht, Nijmegen, 1929. Reprinted in *Selected writings of Edward Sapir in language, culture, and personality,* pp. 206-12. Berkeley: University of California Press, 1949.

Skinner, B. F. Has Gertrude Stein a secret? *Atlantic Monthly,* 1934, 153, 50-57. Reprinted in *Cumulative record: A selection of papers.* 3rd ed., pp. 359-69. Englewood Cliffs, NJ: Prentice-Hall, Inc., 1972.

Skinner, B. F. The verbal summator and a method for the study of latent speech. *Journal of Psychology,* 1936, 2, 71-107.

Skinner, B. F. *The behavior of organisms.* Englewood Cliffs, NJ: Prentice-Hall, Inc., 1938.

Skinner, B. F. A quantitative estimate of certain types of sound-patterning in poetry. *American Journal of Psychology,* 1941, 54, 64-79. Reprinted in *Cumulative record: A selection of papers.* 3rd ed., pp. 391-407. Englewood Cliffs, NJ: Prentice-Hall, Inc., 1972.

Skinner, B. F. *Science and human behavior.* New York: Macmillan, 1953.

Skinner, B. F. *Verbal behavior.* Englewood Cliffs, NJ: Prentice-Hall, Inc., 1957.

Skinner, B. F. *The technology of teaching.* Englewood Cliffs, NJ: Prentice-Hall, Inc., 1968.

Skinner, B. F. *Contingencies of reinforcement: A theoretical analysis.* Englewood Cliffs, NJ: Prentice-Hall, Inc., 1969.

Skinner, B. F. Creating the creative artist. In *On the future of art,* pp. 61-75. New York: Viking, 1970. Reprinted in *Cumulative record: A collection of papers.* 3rd ed., pp. 333-44. Englewood Cliffs, NJ: Prentice-Hall, Inc., 1972.

Skinner, B. F. *Beyond freedom and dignity.* New York: Knopf, 1971.

Skinner, B. F. *Cumulative record: A selection of papers.* Englewood Cliffs, NJ: Prentice-Hall, Inc., 1959, 1961 (enlarged ed.), 1972 (3rd ed.).

Skinner, B. F. *About behaviorism.* New York: Knopf, 1974.

Slobin, D. I. *Psycholinguistics.* Glenview, Ill.: Scott, Foresman, 1971.

Solomons, L. M., and Stein, G. Normal motor automatism. *Psychological Review,* 1896, *3,* 492-512.

Spence, K. W. *Behavior theory and conditioning.* New Haven, Conn.: Yale University Press, 1956.

Staddon, J. E. R. Asymptotic behavior: The concept of the operant. *Psychological Review,* 1967, 74, 377-91.

Stein, G. *Tender buttons: Objects, food, rooms.* New York: Claire Marie, 1914.

Thurman, J. Gertrude Stein. *Ms.,* 1974, 2, 54-57, 93-95.

Tinbergen, N. *The study of instinct.* Oxford, Eng.: Clarendon Press, 1961.

Warren, H. C. *A history of the association psychology.* New York: Scribner's, 1921.

Watson, J. B. *Psychology, from the standpoint of a behaviorist.* Philadelphia: Lippincott, 1919.

Watson J. B. *The ways of behaviorism.* New York: Harper & Brothers, 1928.

Wenner, A. M. Honeybees: Do they use the distance information contained in their dance maneuver? *Science,* 1967, 155, 847-49.

Whorf, B. L. *Language, thought, and reality: Selected writings of Benjamin Lee Whorf.* Cambridge, Mass.: M.I.T. Press, 1956.

INDEX

Absence, 31, 60, 128
Abstraction, definition, 63
Adages, 104
Address, definition, 72
Advice, 35, 36, 98, 104
Aiken, J. R., 36
Alliteration, 112
Allusions, 108
Alphabet, 18
Ambiguity, definition, 147
Amplification, 37
Amplitude, 8
Announcements, definition, 43
Antecedent conditions, 7, 22, 24
Argot, 80, 81
Assertions, definition, 43, 133
Assonance, 112
Audience, definition, 71, 73, 144
Autoclitic, definition, 129
Automatic writing, 141-142
Autonomy, 79
Aversive stimulus, definition, 28
Aversive stimulation, 15, 99
Avoidance, 34, 91
Awareness, 15, 47
Azrin, N. H., 46, 82

Babbling, 87-89
Behavior, definition, 2
Behavior, operant, 6
Bilingualism, 78-80
Blends, definition, 122
Bloomfield, L., 18, 66
Bousfield, W. A., 109
Brown, R., 47, 82
Bruce, D. J., 113
Bryant, M. M., 36

Cant, 80, 81
Carroll, L., 67, 122
Causal account, 3, 4
Causes, 3, 9
Cause-effect relationships, 21
Centralism, definition, 151
Chain, definition, 101
Choosing words, 77, 118, 126
Circumlocutions, 90
Clangs, 112
Classes, 6, 7
Classical conditioning, 12 (*see also* Respondent conditioning)
Cliches, 104
Cluster, definition, 56-57, 101, 107-108
Cofer, C. N., 109
Cognitions, 2, 152

Common accompaniments, 59
Common elements, 56
Competition, among operants, 136
Compliance, 27, 34, 35, 36, 37
Conditioned reinforcer, definition, 28
Conditioned response (CR), 12
Conditioned stimulus (CS), 7, 12, 111, 145
Connotation, 146
Consummatory behavior, 27
Contingency, 7
Control, 3, 27, 117, 128-129, 134, 136-137, 144, 148
Conventions, 52, 54, 69
    conventional way, 26, 41, 133
    conventional covariation, 26, 41, 44, 136
Correspondence, 50, 52, 56
Counting, 104
Covert, behavior, 74, 75, 76, 82, 103, 126, 145, 150-151
    responses, 85, 149-150
    echoics, 85-87, 92
Creativity, 116, 142
Cumulative recorders, 23
Cursing, 40

Davenport, D., 70
Deaf mutes, 150
Defective chains, 105-106
De Laguna, G., 78
Denotation, 43, 146
Deprivation, definition, 7
Differential reinforcement, 9, 68, 82
Dimensions of behavior (*see* Intensive properties of behavior)
Direct quotations, 23-4
Discriminated audience, definition, 77
Discrimination, definition, 62
Discriminative stimulus, definition, 6
Disinterest, 41, 45, 48, 50
Disposition, 21, 37, 75, 129
Distortions, definition, 52, 54, 122
Dolphins, 70, 91
Double entendres, 81
Duration, 5-6, 9

Ebbinghaus, H., 146
Echoic, definition, 82
Electromyography, 23, 150
Elicit, 13, 54, 87, 145
Emotional behavior, 17, 39, 145
English, 18, 19, 54, 66, 78, 79, 95-96, 101, 110-111, 113, 142
Enthusiasm, 77
Ervin, S. M., 79
Escape, 91, 99

Estes, K. W., 47, 48, 82
Estes, W. K., 3
Etymology, 60, 65
Euphemism, 53
Exaggeration, 54
Excursion, 5-6, 9
Experts, 45, 51, 126
Extended tacts, definition, 55
Exteroceptive, 150
Extinction, definition, 17, 68

Fant, C. G. M., 18
Feelings, 126
Ferster, C. B., 150
Findley, J. D., 6
Finnegans Wake, 121, 142
Foley, J. P., Jr., 109
Folk etymologies, definition, 123
Force, 5-6, 9
Formal cluster, definition, 111
Formal overlap, definition, 121
Formulas, 105
French, 19, 20, 66, 79, 81, 85, 87, 110, 113, 123-124
Freud, S., 82, 122
Frisch, K. von, 70
Functional relations, 3, 8

Galton, F., 109
Galvanic skin response (GSR), 110-111
Gardner, B. T., 70
Gardner, R. A., 70
Generalization, 61, 63, 89, 95, 138, 139
    (*see* Stimulus generalization)
Generalized conditioned reinforcer, 46
Generalized mands, definition, 38
Genetic constitution, 3, 87
Gestalt psychology, 4
Goodenough, F. L., 107
Grammars, 2, 105, 107, 128, 152
Grammatical tagging, 134
Gratitude, 15, 34
Greenspoon, J., 46, 47, 82
Guthrie, E. R., 3

Hale, H. E., 78
Halle, M., 18
Haplology, definition, 106
Haveman, E., 18
Hayman, D., 121
Hearers, 10, 61-62, 64, 66, 68, 71, 74, 92,
    102-104, 130-131, 133-134, 136, 144-146
Higginson, F. H., 121, 142
Hildum, D. C., 47, 82
History, 105
Hoijer, H., 69
Holz, W. C., 46, 82
Homans, G. C., 16
Homogeneous chain, definition, 105-106
Homographs, 95
Homonyms, 64-65

Homophones, 95
Honig, W. K., 46, 82
Howes, D., 109
Hull, C. L., 3, 105, 118
Hunger, 5, 7, 9
Hypocorism, 80
Hypothetical constructs, 150
Hysteria, 82

Ideas, 2, 152
Ideal tacts, definition, 52
Idioms, 104
Illiterates, 94
Impure mand, definition, 32
Independent variables, 3
Indirect quotation, 24
Induction, 89, 139 (*see also* Response
    induction)
Inexactness, 52, 54
Innate, 86
Instincts, 86
Intensive properties of behavior, 5-6, 8, 23,
    135, 150
Intent, 15
Interested behavior, 33
Interested tacts, 48
Interlocking verbal behavior paradigm, 13
Intermittent reinforcement, 8, 17, 101-102
International phonetic alphabet, 18, 23
Intraverbal, definition, 100
Intrusion, definition, 122
Invitations, 36
Irony, 81

Jakobson, R., 18, 87
Jargon, 54, 78-79, 80
Jenkins, J. J., 92, 107, 109
Jesperson, O., 78
Johnson, D., 70
Joyce, J., 121, 142
Judson, A. J., 109

Kagan, J., 18
Kaplan, E. L., 87
Kaplan, G., 87
Keller, F. S., 95, 103
Kent, G. H., 109, 112
Kinesthetic feedback (*see* Proprioception)
Kisses, 34
Knowing, 16

Latency, 9
Laugh getting, 54
Lecture audience, 74
Linguistic relativism, 69
Literary audience, 54, 77
Literary words, 96
Lorenz, K., 5, 86
Loudness, 23
Lying, 54

MacCorquodale, K., 2, 66
McGuigan, F. J., 76, 151

Macmillan, Z., 109
McNeil, E. B., 112
Magical mand, definition, 39
Magnitude of reinforcement, 54, 103, 118
Mand, definition, 25
Meaningless word, definition, 146
Meanings, 2, 10, 18, 43, 79, 89, 146
Mediated generalization, definition, 110-111
Mediated operant, 89
Mediator, definition, 16, 26
Mednick, M. T., 110
Metaphor, 57, 61
Metonomy, 59-60, 68, 89
Metonymical extension, 90-91, 97, 134
Miller, G. A., 19, 142
Minds, 2, 3, 148, 152
Misspeaking, 107, 122, 141, 151
Morphemes, definition, 18
Motivation, 31, 50
Motor theory of speech perception, 146
Multiplication, 105

Naming, 42, 43
Native American Languages, 18, 79, 80
Natural science account, definition, 1, 2, 4
Need for achievement, 79
Negation, 133
Negative conditioned reinforcer, definition, 28-29
Negative reinforcer, definition, 8, 28
Negative reinforcement, definition, 29
Neologisms, 25, 67
Nods, 34, 46
Nonnaming tacts, 43, 133
Nonsense syllables, 146
Nonverbal generalized conditioned reinforcers, 46
Nonverbal behavior, 11
Novel stimuli, 55, 68
Number of reinforcements, 103, 118

Object class names, 63, 90
Onomatopoeia, 66
Open frames, 139
Operant behavior, definition, 6
Operant conditioning, 5
Operant level, definition, 87
Operant paradigm, 10, 13
Opposites test, 22
Ordering, 135, 136
Orthography, 95, 97
Oscillatory inhibition, 118
Osgood, C. E., 109
Overworked chain, definition, 105-107

Palermo, D. S., 107, 109
Palmer, A. S., 53, 123
Paradigms, 6, 8, 10-12, 26, 105
Parasitic responses, 38, 104
Parrots, 86, 91
Pats, 34, 46

Pauses, 17, 18, 94
Pavlovian conditioning, 12 (*see* Respondent conditioning)
Pavlovian paradigm, 11-13, 90
Perception, 92
Peripheralism, definition, 151-152
Persistence, 8, 17
Personality, 79
Phenomenology, 149
Phones, 17, 87, 89, 105
Phoneme, definition, 18
Phonemic chains, 89
Phonic method, 97
Phonic Rv's, 95
Phrases, 20
Phrase blends, 122
Physiologists, 9
Plausible reconstruction, 3, 10, 128
Portmanteau words, 67, 122
Positive reinforcer, definition, 8
Positive conditioned reinforcers, 28
Positive unconditioned reinforcers, 27, 28
Pr ( ), definition, 8, 77
Precision in tacting, 63
Preferential reinforcement, 54
Premack, D., 70
Primary operant, definition, 129
Primary tacts, 131
Primary variables (PV), 73-74, 75, 76, 82, 91, 119, 130
Primary verbal behavior, definition, 129
Prior entry effect, 109
Private languages, 80
Probability, 6, 8, 22, 32, 37, 42, 54, 73, 75, 87, 97, 118-119, 139, 150
Probe, definition, 125
Production effect, definition, 23
Projective tests, 37
Promises, 15, 34-35, 37
Prompt, definition, 125
Proper name, 62, 64, 94-96
Properties, 63, 65, 90
Proprioception, 86, 100, 103, 150
Proximity effect, 109
Psycholinguistics, 4
Psychotherapists, 82
Punishment, 77, 91, 145, 149
Pure tact, definition, 45

Quantifiers, 131
Questions, 39

Rapid eye movements (REM), 151
Rapidity, definition, 23
Rappoport, A., 112
Rate, definition, 23
Received American English, 18
Reference, 43, 146
Reflexes, 7, 12, 13, 23, 69
Reinforcement, definition, 8
Reinforcing community, 44-45, 48, 50, 54, 63, 71, 87

Repeated tacting, 63
Repetition, 23
Respondent behavior, 54, 145
Respondent conditioning, 12
Respondents, 110-111
Response, definition, 6
Response competition, 122, 131
Response induction, definition, 39, 114, 139 150
Rhyme, 112
Rosanoff, A. J., 109, 112
Rosenthal, R., 82
Russell, B., 147
Russell, W. A., 109
Rv, definition, 13
Rv:S^D, definition, 100

Salivation, 12, 145
Sapir, E., 79-80
Saturating stimuli, 109
S^{AV}, definition, 28
Schedules of reinforcement, 103, 118
Schoenfeld, W. N., 103
Schoonover, R. A., 76, 151
Scientific audience, 54, 77
S^D, definition, 6
Self-echoics, 86, 91
Self-expression, 50
Self-probes, 126
Self-prompts, 126
Selfridge, J. A., 142
Semantic generalization, 110
Sense data, 68
Serial position, 135
Shakespeare, W., 114, 121, 124
Shaping, definition, 9, 45, 82
Shocks, 29, 31
Simile, 57
Simple conditioned reinforcer, 45
Simple stimulus generalization, 55-56, 110
Skinner, B. F., 1-4, 6, 16, 22-25, 27, 34-36, 38-39, 46, 51, 59, 61-62, 66, 74, 80, 91, 95, 98, 112-114, 121, 126-128, 139, 141-143
Slang, 80
Slips of the tongue, 141
Slobin, D. I., 4
Slurring, 106
Smiles, 34, 46
Social behavior, definition, 16
Solomons, L., 141
Special reinforcement history effect, 109-110
Species specificity, 28, 86
Spelling, 90
Spence, K. W., 3
Spoonerisms, 107
S^R, definition, 8, 27, 28
S^{R-}, definition, 28-29
S$^{R-\cdot D}$, definition 29

S^r, definition, 28
S$^{r\cdot D}$, definition, 14
S^{r-}, definition, 28-29
S$^{r-\cdot D}$, definition, 29
Staddon, J. E. R., 6
Stein, G., 141-143
Stimulus generalization, definition, 39, 55
Stimulus generators, 144-146
Stimulus receivers, 144-146
Stimulus-response psychologies, 2, 3
Strength, of an operant, definition, 8, 22-23
Strengthening, 8
Structural linguistics, 17
Successive approximations, 9, 82
Subaudiences, 76
Subword tacts, 65 ·
Superstitious mand, definition, 39
Supplementary strengthening, 32, 119
Supplementary variables, 51-52, 72
Surrogate audiences, 74, 75
Synecdoche, 58, 61
Synonyms, 64

Tact, definition, 41
Tandem schedules, 150
Tender Buttons, 141
Textual, definition, 93
Thematic Apperception Test (TAT), 54, 79
Thematic cluster, definition, 108
Thematic overlap, definition, 120
Things, 61
Thinking, definition, 149
Tinbergen, N., 5
Topography, 6, 146
Twin languages, 80

Unconditioned negative reinforcer, 28-29
Unconditioned responses (UR), 12
Unconditioned stimuli (US), 12
Understanding, definition, 90, 145-146
Understatement, 53
Unobservables, 51

Verbal aggressiveness, 79
Verbal Behavior, 1, 2, 25, 39, 113
Verbal chains, 98
Verbal clutter, 104
Verbal community, 26, 41, 54, 68
Verbal operant, 21
Verbal summator, 112-113
Vocabulary tests, 22

Warren, H. C., 110
Watson, J. B., 148
Whole-part clusters, 57-58
Whorf, B. L., 69
Withdrawal, 79
Word-association test, 22, 94, 101, 107
Words, 10, 18, 20, 43, 96
Writing, 11, 19, 74
Written mand, definition, 39